I0488782

Maximizing

MPS

Profitability

Copyright © 2017 by Guy Carafone – 2nd Edition

Published by: Beantown Publishing LLC

http://www.beantownpublishing.com

Contents

Introduction

Before we delve into the detailed writing, I'd like to make an opening comment. Unlike so many business books that have been written regarding high level strategies, this book is not *pie in the sky* downward look at business from 10,000 feet. Instead, this is a tactical business book that provides useful insight regarding **how to** efficiently and cost effectively manage a Managed Print Services business. Furthermore, much of what I will be sharing is based on real-life business experience and observations from the ground floor up. Ultimately, my hope is that you are able to leverage some of the shared insight managing your own services business.

The utilization of local dedicated resources to service and support print and copier machines in corporate environments has been a common practice as long as those devices have been available in the marketplace. Shortly after the turn of the century, a new offering was introduced to service and support the above-mentioned devices, namely Managed Print Services (MPS). The difference between the old and new service model, the old represents rudimentary support, while the new represents a significantly more encompassing and sophisticated support offering.

In the old days, managing print products meant dedicated individuals were assigned to large company office buildings and/or business campuses to ensure those devices were in working order and properly equipped and stocked with consumable items, including toner/ink and paper. In more recent times, companies are increasingly signing up for MPS deals. In which case, they completely outsource to a Managed Services Provider (MSP) everything having to do with printing, including equipment ownership and much more. *Noteworthy, I just introduced two very similar acronyms (MPS and MSP), which have very different meanings*. The former represents a service offering, while the latter refers to a service provider. Since I will be repeatedly using both acronyms throughout this writing, it's important to be mindful of the distinction.

In a Managed Print Services deal, the MSP assumes full responsibility for hardware financing and management, as well as the accompanying software, and supplying and managing related consumables, including toner/ink and paper. The MSP is responsible for the following activities: doing discovery of the client's existing environment; designing and deploying an efficient hardware solution; and providing on-going (or steady state) support for the duration of the contract, which is likely to run five years or more. Just like Information Technology (IT) outsourcing, which existed long before MPS offering was introduced to the marketplace, there are two predominant reasons clients decide to outsource printing. First, they determine printing is not a core competence they should be designating capital or human resources. Second, and often more importantly, they are attempting to reduce operating cost.

I'd like to start this journey we are about to take together by making a brief comment on why I chose to organize the book in the given manner. Since this book is about maximizing profitability, one might reasonably expect to jump right into financial details. Having spent approximately one half of my professional career in Finance roles, I can safely state, financial results strictly measure how good or bad a business is doing from a dollars and cents standpoint. It's the operational aspect of the business that matters most. In other words, how efficiently and effectively business gets done. That is precisely the reason the first two parts of this book are devoted to the operational aspects of MPS businesses, with Part I focusing on *Managing Business Operations*, and Part II on *Managing Human Resources*. And finally, in Part III, we will do a deep dive into *Managing the Financials*, which largely tie back to the earlier business operations and human resources discussions.

Before we get into the detailed writing, I'd like to say a little more about the topics we will be discussing. Fundamentally, virtually all service businesses involve managing the following five components: human resources, clients, vendors, assets, and of course the P&L. We're going to drill down fairly deeply into each of these components, in particular contracted Deal P&L management and human resource management. Throughout the book, I will share many real-life examples that have direct or indirect impact on profitability.

As most everyone will agree, the best way to learn is through one's own experiences. The second-best way is from other people's shared experiences, which is precisely what I intend to do with this book, drawing from my own professional experience and lessons learned. Having spent most of my professional career in a wide variety of service operations and financial management positions, I have witnessed firsthand what works well in service businesses, and what does not work well and not worthwhile committing resources or investing capital. That said, I intend to share insightful dos and don'ts, as well as best practices I have learned and lived by along the way.

In the first part of the book, we will talk about the core organizational functions that typically make up an MSP business, including Pursuit (Sales), Solution Team, Discovery, Design, Transition, and Steady State. The primary focus of this discussion will be on how these individual organizational units can work smarter and more efficiently. We will then talk about the overhead functions typically included in an MSP organization, consisting of Business Operations, Business Analysis, and Global Functions (applicable to worldwide businesses). Regarding overhead resources, the focus will be on whether or not all of those resources are truly required and justifiable on the basis of return value. And finally, we will talk about managing three other aspects of MPS businesses, including clients, vendors, and assets.

The second part of the book will involve a fairly detailed discussion regarding human resource management. Incidentally, no matter what type of service business we choose to discuss, service is essentially a people cost business. Therefore, how human resources are justified and utilized will invariably have a significant impact on the bottom line. That is the reason this part of the book is entirely dedicated to managing multiple aspects of human resources. We will start by talking about justification required for existing, replacement, and additional resources. We will then have an in-depth discussion regarding human resource cost versus return value measurement and management, as it applies to both direct and indirect labor resources. And finally, we will talk about when it makes more sense to use external instead of internal resources.

In the third part of the book, we will do a deep dive into Profit & Loss (P&L) management, in particular contracted Deal P&Ls. To be clear, our primary focus will be on Deal P&L management dos and don'ts. We will talk about the shortcomings and challenges associated with the Plan of Record (POR) P&L. I am referring to the approved Deal P&L budget. We will then have a very detailed discussion about Actual Deal P&L management, including the criticality of financial integrity and having a good understanding of transaction source data. Most importantly, we talk about how Deal P&L managers can leverage available levers and knobs to improve deal profitability. Then we will discuss what Deal P&L managers can do to increase contracted deal size and scope. And finally, we will talk about Deal P&L Forecast best practice processes and tools.

It's important to be mindful of the following fact regarding MPS profitability management. Although the total business may be profitable, does not mean each of the contracted deals in the portfolio is profitable. As a matter of fact, the opposite is generally true. Therefore, having the ability to produce and analyze deal level P&Ls allows managers to make better informed decisions regarding challenging deals. In other words, give the manager the ability to isolate unprofitable deals and do everything reasonably possible to turn those deals around. At minimum, do not renew those deals when the current contract term expires. The fact of the matter, it's one thing to knowingly engage in an initially unprofitable deal that you sincerely believe can turn profitable during the term of the contract. It's an entirely different matter, and totally unforgiving, to renew a known unprofitable deal.

Part I

Managing Business Operations

Chapter 1

Managing Core Business Functions

In this first chapter we'll get into details regarding a typical MSP organization core business functions, including: Pursuit (Sales), Discovery and Design, Transition, and Steady State. The primary focus of our discussion will be on how these organizational units can work better and more efficiently.

Deal Pursuit (Sales) and Solution Team

Like most other businesses, MPS business development starts with Pursuit (Sales). However, unlike most other businesses, pursuing MPS deals is generally a lengthy and costly process. And, after all the time and money spent chasing a deal, there is no guarantee the pursuit will materialize into a sale, meaning a signed service contract. The reason being, competition to win (especially large deals) is typically intense. Furthermore, savvy clients who are masters at vendor management will play competitors against one another to get the best possible deal and price. In any event, once the pursuit evolves into a deal bidding process, that's when the fun begins for the Solution team. Or, should I call it what it really is, a stressful competitive exercise.

The Solution team that is on point for winning deals minimally consists of the following three individuals: salesperson, solution architect, and opportunity consultant (the finance person). Big deals often involve other participants such as the transition manager and delivery and/or client manager that is designated to subsequently manage the deal. Really big or strategic deals will often involve an executive sponsor who is responsible for the high-level relationship with the client. For obvious reasons, these executives do not participate in the day-to-day solution process. However, they are kept informed regarding deal developments and pulled into the process to address high level matters and/or contract negotiation obstacles.

The solution phase is the riskiest part of an MPS engagement. The reason being, it sets the stage for what and how services will be delivered. In many cases, the Solution team is forced to make undesirable compromises. One of the most common is having to agree to non-standard deliverables that the delivery organization is not equipped to handle. Needless to say, this is the kind of thing that causes considerable angst for delivery management. The reason being, they will be forced to make process changes to accommodate the non-standard deliverables, which can be costly and cumbersome. The fact of the matter, in order for the Solution team to remain in a competitive pursuit, they often have to agree to non-standard deliverables. Incidentally, an alternative that sometimes works with motivated clients, is offering them something in return for agreeing to standard deliverables. Most of the time that means offering a lower contract price or other financial incentives.

Discovery and Design

Prior to engaging into a contractual agreement, the MSP would naturally want to know as much as possible about the actual scope and potential risks and challenges associated with the deal. The reason that's important, MSPs are typically locked into long-term contracts that can run five or more years. In which case, they could easily find themselves neck deep dealing with unanticipated challenges throughout the life of the deal. That is precisely the reason signed MPS agreements are normally preceded by a due diligence phase. That means discovery specialists inspect a representative sample of the client's existing environment, which typically consists of approximately 10 - 25% of the total environment. Worth noting, discovery findings often represent one of the most significant factors influencing deliverables that are incorporated in the contractual agreement. Bottom line, the more the service provider knows about the client's existing environment, the lower the potential risk and the element of surprise.

After the contract is signed, the MSP typically proceeds to discover essentially 100% of the client's existing environment, which serves as the foundation for designing the new environment. In other words, design specialists will utilize that information to create the most efficient design possible, including selecting optimal hardware type, size, and placement. By the way, the reason I stated "essentially 100%", there are situations in which dispatching on-site discovery specialists simply does not make economic sense. For example, let's assume your company just won an MPS contract with a large international banking client that has hundreds of identical bank branches located throughout the country. Clearly, there is no point doing a visual inspection of all those bank branches. Inspecting a couple of typical branches should be adequate for developing a design solution for all the branches. From a logistical and cost effectiveness standpoint, discovery is typically done by locally available internal shared resources or external resources hired from local temporary agencies.

Design usually goes hand and hand with discovery. As a matter of fact, the two functions are often combined into a single organization under the same management. Depending on the size and complexity of the deal, design specialists will either work from customer sites and/or a centralized remote location. The effort involved in the design phase is more technical and time consuming than discovery, which is the reason design specialists are higher paid professionals than discovery personnel. For the most part, design is done by internal shared resources who move from account to account in the early stage of contracted deal life cycle. However, there are occasions when design specialists are brought back into the deal as a result of a significant change that may have occurred in the client's environment after the initial deployment.

Noteworthy, when clients are directly involved in day-to-day design decisions, you should expect the process to take more time and be more costly. Furthermore, client organizations run the full gamut from being well-organized and efficient to being overly bureaucratic and inefficient. It goes without saying that an MSP would prefer to deal with a well-organized client. If it's apparent the MSP will be dealing with a dysfunctional client, the best way to protect themselves is by co-creating a governance agreement with the client outlining specifically how they will work together, which should help alleviate potential downstream issues and challenges. To be clear, a governance essentially represents agreed upon rules of engagement between the MSP and the client. Without a governance, the MSP stands to lose the most. From a best practices standpoint, it's always a good idea to have a governance in place, regardless of the type of client the MSP is engaged.

There are two primary factors that influence the amount of time and cost involved in the design phase. The first factor is the number of revisions involved in the design. The more design revisions the greater the cost, which is precisely the reason MSPs need to solidify the decision making process with the client beforehand. I have witnessed some extraordinary situations in which the final design solution took seemingly forever because bureaucratic or fragmented client organizations were involved in the decision making process. You will want to do everything reasonably possible to avoid or minimize these senseless costly revision cycles. The second factor, the more design work done on client sites, the greater the MSP's cost. With continued advancements in tools and technology, design work can largely be done from remote Design Centers, which is considerably less costly than dispatching design specialists to multiple client sites.

Deployment (Transition)

Moving on down the contract life cycle, next comes the deployment (or transition) phase. Similar to discovery and design professionals, transition managers are typically shared resources that move in and out of deals during the early stage of the contract life. In unusual circumstances, such as a client who has a large and complex environment that is in a constant state of flux, a transition manager may be assigned to the dedicated account team for an extended period of time.

During the deployment phase, the transition manager typically possesses the dominant role on the deal management team, while the delivery and/or client manager maintain relatively passive roles. The transition manager is the person responsible for product installation and configuration, as well as dealing with any product availability issues that may arise. It's not uncommon for highly sought-after products to be on allocation. In which case, the transition manager is also responsible for negotiating with product sourcing personnel on matters such as partial release or accepting suitable substitute product. After the deployment is completed, the transition manager relinquishes the dominant role, which is transferred to the delivery or client manager, at which point his involvement in the deal will usually cease.

From a client relationship standpoint, the people skills and professionalism displayed by the transition manager can have a significant impact on the long-term relationship with the client. In order to be successful, the transition manager obviously needs to possess sound technical skills. Equally important, he needs to possess good people (client relationship) skills. I have worked with good and bad transition managers and will tell you that the ones that lack people skills or, worse yet, regularly butt heads with the client, are almost never successful. Generally speaking, clients are more tolerant of resources that may lack some technical skills than those that lack diplomacy. On several occasions, I have witnessed clients demand replacement of skilled transition managers whom the client simply could not tolerate their behavior.

Steady State Support

The last, and by far longest, phase of an MPS contract life cycle is commonly referred to as steady state support. Depending on the size and scope of the deal, steady state can look very different from one deal to another. For example, a small MPS deal is typically handled by a shared delivery manager that remotely supports multiple deals. In those cases, it's not unusual for the delivery manager to never even see the client's physical environment or, for that matter, have face-to-face interactions with the client. Beyond any on-site repair or routine maintenance that may be required on the client's hardware, all other support is generally handled remotely. On the other hand, large, complex deals are usually assigned a dedicated steady state support team. The team typically includes a delivery and/or client manager, as well as a dedicated team of technical and/or other specialty resources. Also, it's not unusual for those big deals to receive some shared resource support from a centralized delivery organization.

Incidentally, continued use and value of technical and/or specialty resources assigned to these big deals should periodically be reevaluated. The reason being, as the deal progresses through the long steady state phase, special needs that may have been necessary in early stage steady state may no longer be needed in later stages. Let's consider the following scenario. Shortly after the client's new hardware environment is set up, let's assume some streamlining opportunities have been identified. The related issues may have been caused by an initial faulty design, or subsequent changes that occurred in the client's business. In any event, a resource that specializes in maximizing hardware utilization will likely have to be brought on board for a limited period of time. Let's assume the work begins and ends during year two of a five-year contract. If that specialty resource is kept on board longer than one year, the incremental cost of carrying him will most likely be greater than the incremental value realized from subsequent relatively smaller improvements that individual participates. Therefore, releasing that individual after one year of service would most likely be the best course of action.

Next, let's talk about the principal customer interface and P&L owner of MPS deals. For small, medium, and moderately large deals, that person would typically be the delivery manager, who is also responsible for overseeing all of the day-to-day account activities, as well as pursuing opportunities that grow the size and scope of the deal. In very large (often referred to strategic deals), a client manager is also assigned to the deal management team. In which case, that person assumes the role of principal customer interface and designated Deal P&L owner. That individual is also responsible for pursuing any upselling opportunities that may exist. Meanwhile, the delivery manager is relegated to strictly focus on overseeing the day-to-day account activities.

Now let's talk about on-site service for MPS deals, which represents a major cost factor. Most MPS deals include bundled hardware. Since hardware is typically financed via embedded leases, the Managed Services Provider is officially considered the lessee, and is therefore responsible for the hardware on-site service cost. That said, who actually provides the on-site service could matter a great deal from a profitability perspective. Generally speaking, the MSP has the following three options.

First, let's assume the MSP represents a Business Unit (BU) within a large product company, which has an internal service and support organization they can leverage. In this case, the MSP BU must be particularly careful not to be overburdened with overhead cost, which is commonplace in large bureaucratic internal service and support organizations. Therefore, it behooves the MSP BU to engage in a fair and equitable agreement with the internal service organization. Otherwise, they may end up with a convenient yet costly support solution that will unduly burden the MSP BU profitability, as well as negatively impact their contracted Deal P&Ls.

The second option, the MSP can set up its own on-site service organization. In this case, the business size and geographical disbursement of the hardware matters a great deal. This option can potentially work under two circumstances. One, the size of the MSP business must be fairly substantial. Two, if the business is relatively small, the hardware must be concentrated within limited geographic areas. The reason being, the more dispersed the hardware, the greater the amount of travel time and cost. For all intents and purposes, travel time has essentially the same impact on a business as idle time. Meaning, the more travel time involved, the more costly and inefficient will be the on-site service organization. And, the more consequential will be the impact on the P&L.

The third option, the MSP can utilize third party on-site service vendors. When done thoughtfully, third party support solutions can be advantageous and cost effective. Regardless of whether third party service represents a stand-alone on-site solution, or they are used to augment internal service and support capabilities, their use can certainly be beneficial. A classic service and support model is using internal on-site resources in concentrated business campuses and urban areas, and utilizing third party vendors for sparsely populated areas. The number one concern regarding the use of third-party service companies is their ability to deliver consistent high-quality service. Therefore, the MSP must do everything reasonably possible to ensure the quality level is as good as their internal service resources deliver. In which case, it may mean incurring some extra third-party monitoring and/or training cost.

Chapter 2

Managing Overhead Business Functions

Too much overhead can be detrimental to an organization, particularly from a profitability standpoint. That is true for a company in its entirety, as well as organizations or business units within a company, such as an MSP BU. There are several overhead functions that are typically included in an MSP organization. The three most common include: Business Operations, Business Analysis, and in global businesses a Global Management Function. We are going to broadly discuss the responsibilities of each of these functions, with particular emphasis on whether or not all of the individuals in those functions are truly necessary and justifiable on the basis of cost vs. return value.

Business Operations

Business Operations is an overhead function that exists in most major organizations or business units. They are typically responsible for the following: creating and updating business processes and procedures, monitoring and reporting key performance indicators, administering customer satisfaction surveys, and a host of other administrative duties. Oftentimes, Business Operations also becomes the *dumping ground* for undesirable admin work, which is offloaded by the other workgroups within the organization or business unit.

As the saying goes, "give someone a crutch and they will come to permanently depend on it." Meaning, once another workgroup has handed off admin work to Business Ops, good luck trying to give it back to the original owner. In business, undesirable admin work is a bit like a hot potato. No one wants to get stuck holding it. Also, when offloading admin work is permitted by management, it will generally stifle business process improvements. Why, you might ask? Because there is no incentive for the original owner to improve processes if they can simply unload undesirable work.

So, how do you effectively address a situation like the one just described? In the first place, don't allow admin work to be easily offloaded. The fact of the matter, if the owner of the admin work does not have any skin in the game, you should expect the undesirable behavior to continue in the future. The simple reason, the owner has nothing to lose and everything to gain from a workload standpoint. The best way to control this behavior is by requiring the workgroup that is seeking help to give something back to Business Ops. In business, one of the best ways to handle that is through the so-called *cost relief process*. In other words, cross charge the workgroup cost center that is receiving support, and credit the Business Ops cost center for the cost incurred providing the support. That way, you are infusing some pain (accountability) into the process, which is almost guaranteed to result in more responsible future behavior. On the other hand, giving those workgroups a pass, by allowing them to offload undesirable admin work without consequences, is simply not smart business.

Business Analysis

Unlike Business Operations, standalone Business Analysis functions are relatively less common. In many cases, business analysis is handled by Business Operations. Nevertheless, it's fair to say, somewhere within the organization, business analysis undoubtedly does occur. It may involve such things as:

analyzing what is happening in the marketplace, what competitors are doing, volume and/or profitability analysis for a particular client(s), etc.

Broadly speaking, I would characterize Business Analysis as a function that is focused on improving business processes and profitability, which is oftentimes done hand and hand with the Finance organization. Incidentally, there is no one best way of integrating business analysis into an organizational structure. It's simply a matter of preference and what management believes will work best in their individual circumstance. That said, I will tell you from personal experience, when a dedicated team of highly qualified and experienced analysts is justifiable, they can often work wonders to improve business processes and profitability.

There are two important factors that will influence success in a standalone Business Analysis team. First, the team manager must be a formidable member of the senior management staff. The reason being, if the function is buried elsewhere within the organization, it will likely not receive sufficient senior management attention to be successful. The second factor, team members must be willing to embrace the notion of self-dissolving. Meaning, if and when their value dwindles below their carrying cost, they must be willing to let go instead of struggling to hang on to simply protect their jobs. That is particularly true for the team manager, who sets the example for the rest of the team. Incidentally, if the team is eventually dissolved or, more likely, reduced in size, there are almost always other positions available elsewhere within the company for proven high-performance individuals.

Allow me to share a real-life example of how a relatively small high performance business analysis team actually functioned, which, incidentally, I was a member. The team was led by a relentless no-nonsense manager, and team members were empowered to do whatever was reasonably possible to improve business performance and profitability. Of course, that did not mean running around *willy-nilly* throughout the organization we supported creating angst and disruption. We definitely worked within a pre-defined framework and regulated guidelines. Furthermore, the projects we tackled were prioritized along with business management involvement and support. In other words, we made sure invested parties were *all in* before we tackled a project.

Since this team supported a relatively new business unit that was struggling with profitability challenges, our primary focus was in the following three areas. First, generate volume and statistical analysis reports regarding key aspects of the business, including accompanying customer level details. Second, identify troubled areas in the business, in particular unprofitable contracted deals. The analytical process usually started with a deep data dive, often down to transaction level detail, followed by the development and execution of short-term and/or long-term improvement plans. In some cases that led to changing business processes, and in a few other cases led to spearheading business policy changes. And finally, our third focus was developing tools and processes that improved the way business was managed. For example, we created and rolled out an intuitive and integrated contracted deal forecasting tool to improve a business process that was clearly lacking.

There were four things about this particular team that made it effective. One, there was a singular overarching focus, namely, improving profitability. Two, the team consisted of business-savvy and knowledgeable individuals who possessed a great deal of operations and/or financial management experience, and were well respected by the management team. Three, the team was fully empowered to do whatever was deemed appropriate and necessary to improve financial performance. And four, the team was led by a no-nonsense manager that was part of the BU senior management team.

If a high impact team like the one described can be effectively integrated into a struggling company or BU you are involved, there is a high probability that team will generate worthwhile results. However, it is absolutely essential team members be empowered and given the required latitude to be successful. To be clear, just because this particular set-up worked well for us does not mean it's the only viable organizational solution. There are other equally effective ways of integrating business analysis into a company or BU. However, there are three fundamental ingredients that must minimally be present to be successful, including: crystal clear focus, high quality analysts, and management support. Without any of those basic ingredients, the chance of succeeding is dramatically reduced.

Now I'd like to talk about a potential downside of business analysis, something commonly referred to as *analysis paralysis.* The fundamental question that must always be asked about the analysis, when is enough enough? The answer will generally depend on the trade-off value of pursuing deeper level questions and answers. Sometimes it's reasonable to just scratch the surface to get the required answer. Other times, the business needs to ascertain a deeper understanding beyond a rudimentary answer. In which case, it may well be worthwhile pursuing progressively deeper level questions and answers. On the other hand, here is what unfortunately often happens in business. You are working for a particularly anal-retentive manager that has an obsession for details. Even though there is no legitimate business reason to analyze additional details, your manager will have you drilling down to the center of the universe (so to speak) seeking unjustifiable answers simply to satisfy his eccentric needs. That is a classic example of analysis paralysis. In other words, expending a great deal more unjustifiable time and effort pursuing answers that are totally unnecessary. Following is a real-life analysis paralysis example, which I would like to share with you.

Before we get into the example details, I'd like to state that I wholeheartedly believe in business analysis, and buy into the basic notion of data driven decision making. However, in this particular case, I want to illustrate how easy it is to go completely overboard, effectively resulting in nothing more than a lengthy wheel spinning exercise. Along with one of my peers, we were directed to go through an analytical exercise, which had to do with a particular business function. Just as with most other large companies, we ran our business on robust business application systems, which meant we had an incredible amount of data available at our fingertips. Our mission was to turn a specific data set into useful information that could be leveraged to make better informed business decisions in the future. The details of the analytical exercise are not important. I'm strictly focusing on the process and the duration of this exercise.

Over a period of three months, the two of us sliced and diced the same data set numerous different ways, attempting to establish a cause-and-effect relationship among the various data elements. To be clear, I'm not talking about a full-time three-month project. This was one of several projects the two of us were handling at that time, which consumed approximately 20% of our collective time during that period. Although my associate and I believe that we arrived at a few reasonable conclusions from analyzing the data, our manager was never satisfied. One after another, our conclusions were rejected until a final decision was made by our manager to abandon the analytical project.

I am not going to be judgmental here and say we were right and our manager was wrong or vice versa. However, I will say, this exercise took much too long and wasted many precious cycles, which, in the final analysis, accomplished absolutely nothing. In retrospect, our time could have clearly been spent on doing something more useful. Fundamentally, once an analytical exercise is brought to a reasonable conclusion, it should be deemed complete and the people involved should move on to the next project. Unfortunately, an anal-retentive manager will often decide otherwise. Meaning, he will require the analysts to continue digging wider and deeper for no apparent reason other than satisfying his own curiosity. Clearly this is wasteful behavior that must somehow be contained in business.

Global Functions

Businesses that are limited to national or local geographical scope do not have to deal with the global issues and challenges I am about to describe. Lucky for them! Whereas, in global companies, there are typically overarching global management functions. So, the question becomes, how much authority should those global management functions have? In a typical global company, the organizational components are broken down into business units. For example, a high-tech product company might have three Product BUs and a Service & Support BU. Depending on the type of products the company produces and sells, they may also have a Managed Services BU.

Nevertheless, these Global BUs will almost always have a Global Functions layer included in the organizational design. For example, a Managed Services BU might have the following global functions embedded within the organization: Global Delivery, Global Finance, Global Sales, Global Marketing, etc. That said, the underlying question becomes, are these global functions helping or hindering the region/country organizations?

From what I have observed, when global functions get too involved in day-to-day region/country affairs, they often create confusion, duplicity, and to a large extent represent an unnecessary cost burden. That's not to say global functions do not serve a useful purpose. Of course they do, but sometimes they simply get in the way. Let's face it, most business is done locally, meaning within a given country or region. Typically, it's the region/country manager who is responsible for the local business, the people, and the corresponding P&L. If that's true, what is the value based reason for having BU global functions? The right answer is provide the regions/countries process and procedure guidelines, which ensure global consistency in the manner the company deals with its customers and delivers business solutions. The wrong answer is meddling too deeply in region/country business affairs. I've seen the latter occur far too often, and will tell you it's never a healthy situation. As we all know, meddling is done by people. Therefore, the more people there are in a global function, the more meddling you can expect to occur.

Allow me to share with you a recent real-life example of a global function that morphed and grew disproportionate to the rest of the Managed Services BU. In this case, I am referring to the Global Delivery function. Previously, Global Delivery was reasonably staffed and limited to providing region/country oversight, which is precisely what they should have continued doing. Instead, they meddled more and more into region/country affairs. Here is what happened in this case. Each year we created the annual Region/Country Budgets, there was an ever-growing cost allocation to the P&Ls for the Global Delivery Function. Meanwhile, all the Region/Country organizations, including the one I worked, were doing everything reasonably possible to preserve and improve gross margin. In other words, protect the portion of the P&L the region/country managers had direct control.

On the other hand, allocated cost below gross margin kept growing each year, effectively eroding any margin gain the region/country managers might have been able to generate. Most of the allocated overhead cost increase was coming from a single organization. You guessed it, Global Delivery. Meanwhile, there was no noticeable incremental value coming back to the BU for the additional overhead cost. As a matter of fact, the opposite was true (more on this in a few moments). Keep in mind, in most global companies the BU Global Functions staff, led by Global Finance, is ultimately responsible for the final Worldwide BU Budget. The region/country managers can complain about the elements of the P&L they don't like, such as ever-growing revenue challenges and overhead allocations. But, those complaints are almost sure to fall on deaf ears. In the public sector, that would be like the State Government telling the Federal Government they will not accept financial responsibility for Federal mandates. Good luck with that!

What was even worse in the situation just described, we constantly felt the ever-growing presents of Global Delivery. In other words, they were meddling more and more into region/country business affairs, which was clearly outside their original mandate. Before we knew it, Global Delivery personnel became entrenched in the individual account review process, demanded strict monthly reporting requirements, and more. In retrospect, the new requirements essentially amounted to nothing more than busywork, which was seemingly done to satisfy Global Delivery curiosity instead of helping advance the business.

Let me share with you a of couple vivid examples of what I am referring. But first I'd like to say, preparing for account reviews takes a great deal of time away from the account manager, whose primary responsibility is overseeing everyday client needs. At the country/region level, account reviews were done in accordance with pre-defined parameters and cadence guidelines, which were principally based on the size of the gap between plan versus actual financial results. Simply put, the greater the gap, the more frequent the required reviews. For especially troubled accounts, reviews were done on a monthly or quarterly basis. Accounts that were moderately off from plan were reviewed on a half year basis. And accounts that were achieving or exceeding plan were reviewed once/year. Admittedly, having to prepare and participate in all of these account reviews may sound a little counterproductive. Especially considering the amount of precious time they take away from account managers. The fact of the matter, there is no other more effective way of placing necessary pressure on account managers to improve contracted deal performance.

Although not perfect, the country/region level account reviews were reasonably effective. However, that did not matter to the BU Global Function managers, who began to request their own reviews, subjecting the same account managers to more unnecessary work. By the way, the work does not end with preparing and delivering the additional account reviews. Invariably, there were several performance related questions asked by the worldwide audience, which required additional analysis and follow-up responses. There is no polite way to say this. Those reviews resulted in wasted cycles that essentially did nothing to address meaningful performance issues that were not already addressed in the country/region reviews. Meaning the additional reviews and corresponding follow-up work amounted to nothing more than satisfying worldwide management curiosity. Long story short, we finally convinced the BU Global Functions to join the country/region level reviews instead of hosting their own reviews, which they eventually reluctantly agreed.

The second example has to do with publishing monthly account performance dashboards. If you're not familiar with business dashboards, they typically operate on the same principle as green/yellow/red street lights. Meaning green represents good performance; yellow represents marginally off performance; and red represents troubled accounts that require immediate attention. We already had a region/country account dashboard reporting system in place, which the worldwide team was included in the distribution. But that was not good enough. Once again, in their infinite wisdom (sarcasm), the worldwide team developed a considerably more complicated account dashboard, which the reporting criteria were fundamentally different from what the regions/countries were using. In the final analysis, there was nothing about the worldwide mandated dashboard that provided any additional benefit. It amounted to nothing more than a nicely formatted PowerPoint presentation document. Incidentally, those documents were much harder to work with than the Excel spreadsheets we previously used, which the data was simply copy/pasted into PowerPoint documents.

In the final analysis, the BU Global Functions impacted the region/country businesses in the following manner. First, they burdened the Region/Country P&Ls with ever-growing cost allocation. Second, they increasingly meddled in region/country business affairs. Third, they consumed precious region/country resource cycles on matters that did nothing to truly advance the business. Bottom line, I am not suggesting BU Global Functions do not serve a useful purpose because they do. They are especially useful establishing and maintaining global consistency in the manner in which region/country businesses operate and deliver client services. On the other hand, I am suggesting they need to be held accountable for bringing tangible value back into the organization. Furthermore, there must be ironclad controls in place to prevent Global Functions from growing at will.

Chapter 3

Managing Other Aspects of MPS Business

Equally important to cost effectively managing internal organizations, MPS businesses must also manage other critical aspects of their business, including clients, vendors, and assets. We're going to discuss each of those three factors in more detail below. In the meantime, it's important to be mindful, how each of those factors is managed will definitely have P&L implications. Incidentally, with regard to assets, besides the impact consumable and/or depreciable assets have on the P&L, how effectively those assets are managed obviously also have Balance Sheet implications. Given the latter is outside the scope of this book, I will not elaborate further on matters having to do with the Balance Sheet.

Managing Clients

One of the fundamental questions regarding effectively managing an MPS business: is the Managed Services Provider managing the client or is the client managing the MSP? A balance of give and take between the two parties will almost always produce the best results. Whereas, an imbalance either way is sure to create angst for the party being overpowered. Some clients are an absolute delight to manage. They are respectful, understanding, and most of all reasonable about demands and expectations from the MSP. On the other hand, some other clients, even relatively small and insignificant clients, can be a handful. Meaning, they expect absolute and immediate attention, as if they are the only client the MSP is doing business.

Then of course you have large strategic clients, who are typically multi-national companies that are experts at vendor management. They know how to play the game (so to speak) to their advantage, beginning with the deal bidding process and continuing throughout the life of the contract. They know how to effectively pit competing MSPs against one another to obtain the best possible deal and price. And, they know how to negotiate price reductions and/or concessions during the life of the deal. These strategic clients often take the following position: "If you want to continue doing business with us or expect future business, your best bet is to give us what we are requesting."

Incidentally, these are the very same clients who routinely escalate matters to their company executives, who in turn have no reservation whatsoever reaching out to the MSP executive sponsor. When that happens, everyone on the MSP side starts jumping through hoops, which is a very inefficient way of addressing business issues that could have otherwise been handled through normal processes. Talk about angst! These actions definitely create anxiety for the MSP client manager and/or delivery manager who may rightfully believe the negative exposure to executive management will adversely affect future career advancement opportunities.

I'm not suggesting all large strategic clients operate in this manner. However, I will tell you many of them do, which is one of the reasons so many of those accounts are marginally profitable for the MSP. Sure, those accounts help increase the top line, but in most cases, do little to contribute to the bottom line. From my point of view, except in rare circumstances, generating unprofitable revenue is bad business, pure and simple. Some people believe in the following twisted notion. You can sign marginally profitable strategic deals and subsequently turn them profitable once the deals are up and running. Without question, some challenging deals can be turned around, but not without a considerable amount of effort. And, in many cases, require making adjustments to standard business processes. The fact of the matter, given the exceptional vendor management skills most strategic account possess, the MSP will more likely have a difficult enough time actually achieving and maintaining the relatively low deal solution margin.

On the other end of the spectrum, most MPS portfolios generally include a significant number of small and medium size deals. Except in unusual circumstances, those accounts are relatively easier to manage and typically more profitable. As a matter of fact, from a profitability perspective, it's not unusual for the small and medium deals to carry the large strategic deals in the portfolio. The primary reason, since small and medium accounts cannot leverage size, they typically don't even bother trying to negotiate non-standard deliverables. A well-known fact regarding Managed Services businesses is the more standard the client deliverables, the more efficient and cost effective will be supporting the deals. Furthermore, many small and medium deals can be supported remotely (at least from a delivery/client management standpoint), allowing the MSP to take advantage of lower labor cost. Bottom line, small and medium deals that have standard deliverables are typically very good for business. Whereas, large non-standard deals tend to be more challenging, often resulting in placing more pressure on profit rather than positively contributing to profit.

Managing Vendors

It's not unusual for Managed Services Providers to deal with multiple vendors, and, in many cases, internal service organizations, which the MSP has a vendor-like relationship. A classic example of the latter is when an MSP represents a BU inside a large product company that has a built-in services infrastructure which the MSP BU utilizes for on-site support. Managed Print Services deals are almost always bundled solutions that include a hardware component, which the MSP is responsible for on-site support. Regardless of whether hardware support is coming from an internal service organization or third-party service providers, there should always be a written agreement between the parties involved. Obviously, agreements with third party service companies represent legally binding contracts. Whereas, agreements with internal service organizations are most likely handled via a non-binding Letter of Intent. Nevertheless, it's always better to have a written agreement to fall back on should the need arise.

One of the most important aspects of third-party service agreements, they often contain a provision that holds the vendor accountable for the same deliverables the MSP is accountable to the end-client. Furthermore, if there are non-performance penalties associated with the MSP and end-client agreement, those same penalties should be incorporated in the MSP and third-party vendor agreement. If those provisions are not included in the latter agreement, shame on the MSP for the omission.

On the other hand, the same handed down non-performance provisions are not likely to be included in an internal Letter of Intent. Instead, agreements with internal service organizations should contain incentives that minimize the number of on-site technician dispatches. Otherwise, there is a distinct possibility the MSP will incur charges from the internal service organization for on-site dispatches that were not truly necessary. One way to control this matter is agreeing to an internal cross-charge rate structure that is based on service resolutions rather than incident dispatches. That way, there is built-in motivation for the internal service organization to be more cost conscience and efficient.

There are of course a number of other types of vendors the MSPs may be involved. One common type is resource vendors, which we will discuss in more detail later. Vendor resources can be leveraged to augment internal resource capability, or provide knowledge and skills that do not exist internally. In any event, it's wise to create a binding agreement between the parties involved that address specific deliverables, milestones, and more.

It's also common for MSPs to incorporate other vendor software/solutions in end-client deliverables. In those cases, the MSP would typically engage directly with the software/solution provider, and pass the cost onto the end-client. Here again, the agreement between the MSP and the software/solution provider needs to be structure is such a way that does not represent undue risk for the MSP. In other words, the software/solution provider must be held accountable if their product does not meet contracted end-client deliverables.

Managing Assets

As previously mentioned, MPS deals are typically handled as bundled solutions, which includes hardware that is financed via embedded leases. To reiterate, an embedded lease is an agreement between the financing company, or financing arm of the product company, and the Managed Services Provider (not the end-client). Given the contractual responsibilities for embedded leases, it behooves the MSP to best place the hardware in the client's environment and know the whereabouts of all the leased equipment. Otherwise, they will suffer the financial consequences associated with mismanagement.

Furthermore, they need to take appropriate and timely action to return any excess or defective hardware in the client's environment. Losing sight of that equipment, and allowing it to collect dust in some client backroom, can be costly. Instead, the MSP should request a Material Return Authorization (MRA) from the leasing entity as soon as the hardware has been deemed to be excess or defective. Incidentally, the leasing entity has no problem with hardware sitting idle at client sites. The reason being, they will continue billing for the hardware as long as it takes the MSP to realize they have a problem. Meanwhile, the MSP is not receiving any offsetting revenue from the client for the inactive hardware. By the way, although leased hardware is technically not an MSP owned asset, mismanagement of that hardware can certainly turn into an asset management challenge for the MSP.

There is another asset category involved in MPS deals, namely, print toner. Prior to being consumed, toner is treated as inventory (a company asset). Once consumed, the cost of the toner moves from the Balance Sheet to the P&L (cost of sales). Noteworthy, profitability of MPS businesses is largely influenced by how well toner is managed and how efficiently it's consumed. Toner inventory is typically held in one of three places: 1) MSP or printer company warehouse; 2) fulfillment centers, which are typically owned and operated by large office supply companies; 3) emergency stock held at select customer sites. The latter is particularly common in big deals, whereby clients insist on having emergency stock available in select locations.

The primary reason for the client's insistence, they want to protect themselves against potential inventory shortages or shipment delays. The fact of the matter, toner cartridges are very sophisticated devices, which have built-in consumption monitoring capability. In other words, the ability to alert users when toner level is running low. Therefore, there is little to no need for toner inventory to be sitting idle at customer sites. Nevertheless, for customer assurance reasons, particularly in big deals, the MSP will often agree to those contractual demands. To be clear, we're not talking about consigned inventory, which the end-client is financially accountable. Pure and simple, this is MSP owned inventory that is basically out of sight and out of mind. Without getting into too much detail regarding this matter, it's not unusual for the MSP to lose control of that inventory due to misplacement and/or misuse. Therefore, it's important to have proper controls in place before the inventory is distributed to client sites.

Toner that is distributed to end-clients by external fulfillment companies is not considered MSP owned inventory. The reason being, that toner is initially sold and shipped in bulk to the fulfillment companies. When the fulfillment company subsequently receives an order to ship an individual toner to the end-client, an electronic notification is sent to the MSP who treats the toner buyback as cost of sales. In other words, the MSP is basically buying back the toner at an uplifted price, which allows the fulfillment company to recover their cost plus allow an uplift to cover shipping and handling cost and a reasonable profit. I realize this process may sound somewhat convoluted, but it actually works quite well. The other option would be to consign toner to the fulfillment companies, but that would tie up a tremendous amount of inventory for the MSP. Therefore, selling and buying back the toner is the better of the two given choices.

A third way of distributing toner to end-clients is directly from the MSP warehouse. Although this option eliminates the middleman, there is a significant amount of individual toner handling required, which the MSP (or printer company) may prefer not to be involved. The simple reason, they do not consider toner distribution to be a core competence.

Part II

Managing Human Resources

Chapter 4

Justifying Human Resources

Service businesses are largely people cost businesses. Therefore, how those people are justified, measured, and managed matters a great deal from a profitability perspective, which is the reason I devoted the entire second part of the book to the subject matter. First, we're going to talk about justification processes for existing, replacement and additional resources, each having their own unique challenges and one common shortcoming, namely, lacking process rigor. Unfortunately, many companies do not routinely apply sufficient rigor to the human resource justification processes until it's too late. Meaning, they are experiencing financial difficulty, requiring them to tighten their hiring processes.

Instead of being reactive, which oftentimes means doing too little, too late to have *real* impact on the business, we're going to talk about ways to get in front of this challenge to avoid potential downstream consequences. Speaking from extensive personal experience, I can safely state that when companies are in reactive mode, the resource approval process is generally painfully slow. As a result, managers who are in desperate need of replacing critical resources, especially customer facing resources, suffer the greatest consequences. The reason being, delaying replacement of critical customer facing resources will often result in the inability to meet contracted deliverables, which is never a good thing. That is especially true when non-performance financial penalties are involved. Hence, the wise thing to do is treat requests for customer facing replacement resources with a greater sense of urgency.

Justifying Existing Resources

Unless a business is performing particularly poorly, existing resources are ordinarily not re-justified during the annual budgeting process. Instead, those resources are considered part of a baseline budget, which frankly speaking is unfortunate. The reason being, companies are not taking advantage of potential resource cost reduction opportunities that may exist. Typically, as businesses grow and change, so too change their resource requirements. There are numerous reasons resource requirements can change. For illustration purposes, we're going to talk about a couple of common reasons.

First, as a result of business growth, let's assume a company decides to migrate from several disparate business application systems to an integrated enterprise system like SAP. As you might imagine, for most companies this would represent a significant and costly undertaking. Accordingly, they would ultimately expect to yield some efficiency benefits from the investment, including a reduction of Information Technology (IT) resources. If you have ever been involved in a sizable enterprise business application system implementation, you know that they are typically long-term projects, which could easily take two or more years to fully implement. Companies that are implementing these systems usually bring in expert resources from a management consulting firm to guide them and sometimes lead the system configuration and implementation effort. Furthermore, those companies are likely to assign select internal IT resources to the project who will likely subsequently support both the newly implemented system and user community after the rollout.

Generally speaking, the integration of those resources works as follows. Throughout the configuration and implementation phases, select internal IT resources become seamlessly integrated with the consulting resources. Shortly after the system has been rolled out, the consultants move on, leaving only the internal IT resources to support the system and the user community. Since the new system functionality is invariably different from the old disparate systems, there is growing reliance on IT resources from the user community. And before you know it, IT resources are busy helping end-users execute business transactions, running reports, etc. Frankly, much of what occurs is nothing more than handholding (so to speak), until the users become more self-sufficient utilizing the new system.

Given this common development, the following question typically arises. What happened to the original plan of reducing internal IT resources after the new system is implemented? The answer is, activities such as running ad hoc reports, which end-users previously performed on their own, now require IT resource assistance to do the same on the new system. Also, what was considered routine business transactions in the old systems are now causing some users difficulty executing similar transactions on the new system, resulting in IT resources having to help those users. These challenges will eventually dissipate, but it may take the better part of a year before end-users become fully self-sufficient. In the meantime, management is caught squarely in the middle of a classic dilemma.

They could choose to play hardball and reduce the originally planned IT resources, but that would upset the user community. On the other hand, they could continue to have IT resources provide end-users hand holding assistance, but that would result in unbudgeted financial consequences. So, what should management do? The right answer is objectively analyze the situation and take immediate action to minimize dependency on IT resources.

Let's assume management determines IT resources are spending approximately 25% of their time helping end-uses run reports and execute business transactions. In that case, the most likely course of action would be to invest in end-user training, which will make them more self-sufficient and less reliant on IT resources sooner than later. Doing nothing is not a viable option. The reason being, as the saying goes, "provide someone a crutch and they will come to always depend on it." On the other hand, slowly wean the person off the crutch and see how quickly he starts walking on his own again. The same holds true for IT assistance. Meaning, the best approach is to identify and prioritize activities that are causing end-users difficulty, and systematically address those activities with targeted improvement initiatives.

Another common example of missed resource reduction opportunity occurs when business process improvements are implemented. Most companies continuously modify their internal processes to meet ever-changing business needs. Also, many companies routinely look for ways to make existing processes more efficient. The fact of the matter, streamlining business processes represents only partial success. Taking corresponding resource action is equally important. Unfortunately, many companies claim success when process improvements are implemented, and do not take the next logical step to reduce resources that are no longer needed. The reason being, many managers struggle with that next step. They naturally do not want their team members to be out of a job. But, here's the thing. Embracing those unpopular and difficult decisions when they present themselves can potentially circumvent having to deal with much more significant resource decisions when the company's overall success or longevity may be on the line.

Just as new resources need to be justified, existing resources should also periodically be re-justified. I'm not suggesting companies adopt a zero-based budgeting process in order to contain non-essential resource cost. However, I am recommending companies periodically reevaluate resource needs, especially indirect resources. The basic reason, ensure the company continues to receive justifiable return value from those resources. The most effective way to do that is to periodically re-assess the need for the tasks indirect resources are performing, and objectively evaluate the impact to the business if those tasks were to cease. You might quickly come to realize that many tasks that were once considered vital to the business are no longer necessary. For example, on-going reporting and analysis that may have been implemented for a specific need or circumstance that no longer requires constant monitoring.

Oftentimes, new reporting and/or analytical processes are instituted as a result of problems that have occurred in a business. As time passes and notable progress is made resolving those business issues, the reporting and analysis nevertheless routinely continue, even though management is no longer truly paying attention to the matter. So, what should management do in these situations? The first step, identify and eliminate non-essential tasks and consolidate the remaining tasks under fewer individuals. The second step, eliminate resources that are no longer needed. As previously stated, the latter step is not pleasant. Therefore, some managers will shy away from taking those action. On the other hand, managers who are motivated to deliver improved performance are more likely to embrace those actions as an opportunity to positively impact the company's bottom line, as well as improve the likelihood of their own professional growth.

I'd like to make one additional comment regarding containment of existing resource cost. Given that people represent the lion's share of service cost, running a successful and profitable service business is a perpetual balancing act between resource cost management and maintaining desirable customer satisfaction levels. That said, although managers are paid to make business decisions, oftentimes it's the people on the ground, who work directly with customers, that know best. Therefore, my advice is to encourage those people to come forth with process and/or profit improvement ideas, and reward them for ideas that are implemented. It's amazing how many worthwhile ideas can come from individuals who are on the ground, especially ideas that make it possible for organizations to work smarter, faster, and cheaper without sacrificing customer satisfaction. The fact of the matter, besides his or her job skills, every person brings their brain to work every day. So, why not leverage everything they have to offer?

Justifying Replacement Resources

Except during unusually challenging business circumstances, most companies treat hiring of replacement resources as a foregone conclusion. Meaning, if there was good reason for having the position filled before it was vacated, there is good reason to backfill it now. Instead, management should look at every resource replacement as a potential cost reduction opportunity. Sometimes the position being vacated can be replaced with a partial resource. In other cases, management should consider doing the following. Evaluate all of the incumbent's activities and separate them into critical and non-critical categories. Eliminate non-critical activities, and either give the remaining activities to another existing resource or divide them amongst several resources who have available bandwidth.

In other situations, there may be an opportunity to replace the vacated position with a lower job level. Sometimes the existing job level is unduly influenced by the seniority and experience level of the incumbent, instead of the knowledge and skills actually required to do the job. In those cases, it would behoove the hiring manager to backfill the position with a lower level resource or maybe a new college hire. Either way, the work will get done at a lower cost, something managers should always be striving to achieve.

Incidentally, although new college hires typically do not possess a significant amount of experience coming into a new position, they tend to learn and grow rapidly. In many cases, they will give their all in return for being given an employment opportunity. Of course, the same may be true for motivated existing employees who are given advancement opportunities. Nonetheless, there are a number of different approaches the hiring manager can potentially take advantage to reduce replacement resource cost. Bottom line, each situation should be approached with the following two things in mind. Adopt the best solution that fulfills *essential* business needs, and takes advantage of any potential cost reduction opportunities that may exist.

On the other hand, there are situations in which time sensitive client support replacement decisions should be made that are not. Delays could be due to a company's *one size fits all* replacement policy, or a hiring approval manager deliberately dragging his heels. Regardless of the reasons for delays, the results are never good and oftentimes consequential. Sure, a service provider may save some money during the time the replacement position is left vacant, but at what cost? I have been on the receiving end of delayed resource replacement decisions. And, can tell you, it's particularly frustrating for an account manager or delivery manager that is stuck in the middle. The reason being, they are hamstrung by poor internal policies and/or management practices, while still being expected to meet customer deliverables without sufficient resources.

The fact of the matter, customers don't care about the service provider's internal policies and processes. All they care about is ensuring the service provider meets their delivery obligations. When deliverables are not met, there will be consequences. In some cases, it may result in something relatively minor, such as a temporarily dissatisfied customer. In other cases, it could result in something more serious such as a non-performance financial penalty. The point being, customers have a number of different options they can exercise when a service provider is not delivering on their promise. In which case, resource shortages will certainly add to non-performance risk.

The bottom line, resource replacement processes must be sufficiently flexible to meet varying business needs. Whenever a *one size fits all* process is implemented, there will invariably be resulting consequential issues and challenges. Generally speaking, replacing direct labor resources, especially people who are responsible for customer deliverables, need to be treated with a greater sense of urgency than replacing indirect resources. On the other hand, every resource replacement (especially indirect resources) should be viewed as a potential cost reduction opportunity.

Justifying Additional Resources

Justification for additional resources is commonly *need-based*, which in many cases would be more accurately characterized as *want-based* justification. In any event, it's fair to say, need-based justifications do not go through the same rigor as value-based justifications. The latter would involve a comparison of the prospective employee's fully burdened cost to the projected value that individual is expected to bring back to the company. Hiring decisions are considered financially prudent when the projected return value exceeds the individual's fully burdened cost, and imprudent when the opposite is true. With that in mind, let's take a closer look at need-based versus value-based hiring justification.

One factor that will commonly influence the ease or difficulty of getting additional resources approved is the company's current financial condition. When business performance is good, there is typically less rigor applied to the resource hiring process. That means hiring managers have an easier time getting additional resources approved, with or without quantified value justification. Unfortunately, therein lies the problem. Why, you might be wondering? Because the lack of rigor will almost certainly result in hiring too many non-essential resources. In which case, instead of helping businesses advance, those resources often end up doing nothing more than watching over *real* work being done by others. Meaning, doing more counting, analysis, controlling, and other superfluous work. While a reasonable amount of the noted activities is essential in most businesses, too much is a waste of time and money.

Need-based hiring justification is also common when the opposite condition exists. In other words, business performance is not good. In these situations, a hiring manager might convince approving managers that additional analysis and control is precisely what the company needs to get back on track. The fact of the matter, blind faith (non-value quantified) resource approvals are risky at best. Although I must admit, I've seen blind faith hiring go both ways, meaning some proved worthwhile while others did not. I have witnessed situations in which a new hire, such as a financial analyst or controller, turn out to be exactly what was needed to bring challenging business matters under control. The added checks and balances and increased awareness and accountability did wonders to help managers make better informed decisions, which in turn helped advance the business.

I have also seen the opposite occur. Meaning, the added resources increased existing bureaucracy or performed meaningless analysis, which did nothing to help the business. My point being, you can go with blind faith hiring and hope for the best. Or, you can go with a more reliable and less risky value-based approach. As a long-standing people manager, I will tell you there is no comparison between value-based and need-based hiring decisions. Hence, my position on the matter is clear. For the most part, if you want an additional resource, you must justify it on the basis of value. I should also point out that quantifying return value goes beyond just the initial approval process. There is a certain amount of after the fact rigor that must be applied to validate a prudent value-based hiring decision was actually made. Otherwise, it may be necessary to subsequently course correct, which is never pleasant. Especially for individuals whose jobs are on the line, and secondarily for managers who are responsible for taking those actions.

Although I am an advocate of value-based hiring decisions, there are times when you will have no choice but to go with need-based (or faith-based) decisions. Nevertheless, after the fact rigor is always recommended. At this point, I'd like to walk you through a few real-life hiring examples along with corresponding after the fact results. First, I will share two examples of faith-based hiring decisions, which one proved worthwhile and the other did not. Afterward, I will share two examples of value-based decisions, which, here again, one proved worthwhile and the other did not.

One of the Managed Services business units I worked signed a multi-year $100M contract with a large global company to manage and support their entire domestic print environment. The scope of the deal included several campus locations, as well as numerous single office locations across the USA. From the outset, this deal represented a losing proposition. We lost approximately $10M each of the first two years of this seven-year contract. Basically, we were dealing with a runaway situation that was screaming for attention.

After several disappointing executive management reviews, two personnel actions were ultimately taken. First, the client manager was replaced with someone who was more diplomatically forceful and capable of achieving better balance between the client and our BU. Previously, the relationship was very much one-sided, favoring the client. The second personnel action involved adding a knowledgeable and experienced finance manager to the dedicated deal management team. Previously, the deal was supported by a shared financial analyst who was responsible for supporting multiple deals, which meant this deal received minimal attention. Clearly, this was not just another standard deal. It was large and complex, which meant it had to be staffed differently in order for the deal to be successful.

Long story short, the new finance manager delved quickly and deeply into the problem areas and systematically led several successful profit improvement initiatives. After losing approximately $20M during the first two years of the deal life, the bleeding (so to speak) was essentially brought under control. Given the challenging deal solution assumptions that were made, we would never make money on this deal. However, after two disastrous years, we were able to keep the deal running at essentially break-even.

It took the right people with the necessary knowledge and skills to get this deal back on track. Replacing the client manager and, in particular, adding a dedicated finance manager worked wonders to improve the financial performance of this very challenging deal. There was no way to realistically quantify the return value of the finance manager when the resource hiring decision was being made. However, we were confident that the right person with maniacal focus could improve the deal financial performance. Although this was a need-based (or faith-based) hiring decision, the end result definitely proved to be worthwhile.

Incidentally, the hard lesson learned from this particularly challenging deal, investing in a logo (meaning a big-name client) can turn into a very expensive proposition. The fact of the matter, businesses that wish to grow or establish dominance, especially in a competitive environment, will often have to make risky decisions. In this case, the BU decided to invest in one of the big global players in a particular industry sector. The reasoning, if we could successfully win over one dominant player in that industry and do a good job supporting that client, other big players would likely follow. I'd like to make the following comment regarding this idealistic assumption. In business, there is a difference between making a strategic decision and an outright foolish one. In retrospect, given the obvious risk we took and the magnitude of the resulting financial loss, this decision clearly fell into the latter category.

Next, I'd like to talk about the non-worthwhile faith-based hiring decision example. But, before I do, I'd like to make a few comments. In the business world, when something isn't working as planned or anticipated, changes are sure to come. But, here's the thing about changes. Oftentimes, those changes end up being more motion than progress. How many times in your career have you seen changeover from centralized to decentralized management structure? How many times have you seen the exact opposite occur after a new executive manager comes in with his so-called *revolutionary ideas,* which end up fizzling during the implementation phase? How many times have you seen changes in regional management structure, adding or consolidating region managers to an organization? Okay, I'll stop there. My point being, these changes often end up being nothing more than costly motion. Furthermore, in many cases the changes result in unnecessary internal disruption and, even worse, upsetting and confusing customers.

Let's get back to my example. A few years ago, the BU I worked moved from a classic three region structure to five regions within the USA. At that time, revenue was running relatively flat and gross margin was slightly better than break-even, which meant something had to be done to try to improve financial performance. So, guess what happened? In an effort to improve both the top line and bottom line, BU management came up with the grandiose idea of moving from three to five regions, believing that change would somehow improve matters. In retrospect, the change ultimately accomplished nothing more than promote two people to regional manager, which of course also meant adding corresponding overhead expense. Along with the structural change, the regional account portfolios had to be changed, which meant a significant number of customer accounts had to move from one regional portfolio to another.

Incidentally, it didn't end there. In many cases, the five region managers felt compelled to personally reach out to several of their respective high profile and/or highly sensitive clients to provide them assurance they would continue to receive the personal attention they deserved. Based on after the fact results, it's safe to say, after six months of employee and account designation turmoil, there was no measurable improvement in revenue or margin. I am not suggesting organizational realignments such as the one described should never occur. Of course, as businesses grow and change, so too should organizational structures be adjusted to support those changes. But, when there is no growth occurring in the business, expecting revenue and profit to improve by simply expanding the management structure is, how shall I put this? Illusionary!

Now let's discuss the two value-based hiring decision examples, starting with the one that did not prove worthwhile. Generally speaking, as the number of contracts in a service business grows, so too does the requirement for direct labor resources. Similarly, the greater the projected sales volume, the more sales resources are usually required. Following is a common scenario that precipitates hiring additional Sales and Pursuit resources in a Managed Services business unit.

During the annual budgeting process, corporate management challenged the BU to achieve higher sales volume, to which BU management responded with a request for additional Sales and Pursuit resources that would be required to achieve the higher sales volume. One of the most common approaches used to justify additional Sales and Pursuit resources is utilizing a revenue per employee guideline. Without getting distracted by a lengthy discussion regarding typical ever-growing stretch goals, let's assume the current annual revenue per employee is $2M. In which case, if the company wants to grow revenue by $50M, they would have to add 25 Sales and Pursuit resources.

Let's assume the request for an additional 25 Sales and Pursuit resources is approved and those individuals are brought on board. Next, the new fiscal year is kicked off with a grand and costly National Sales meeting. Everyone comes out of the Sales meeting fired up and ready to tackle their aggressive sales quotas. Shortly thereafter, reality sets in.

As they approach the end of the 1st quarter, Sales signals they will not make their Q1 numbers. But, there is no need to panic. They'll make up the Q1 shortfall in the subsequent quarters. So, they add the Q1 shortfall to the Q2 – Q4 forecast, demonstrating they will still achieve the total year budget. What do you think happens next? You guessed it! The end of Q2 is approaching, and Sales once again signals they will not make the Q2 numbers. Now they are facing a real dilemma. What should they do? Depending on the size of the shortfall and the probabilities assigned to deals in the sales funnel, they can do one of two things. Spread the Q2 shortfall into the Q3 and Q4 forecast, or concede they will not achieve the total year budget by adjusting down their total year forecast. Either way, at this point management concern is certainly elevated. If Sales goes with the spread approach, they will be given a reprieve for one additional quarter. If they go with dropping the total year forecast, they will surely face pressure to find ways to correspondingly reduce cost in order to preserve as much gross margin as reasonably possible.

In organizations like Sales and Pursuit, there is only so much cost you can squeeze out by cutting down travel, slowing down purchases, and taking other marginally beneficial cost cutting actions. *Real* cost reduction will only be achieved by reducing the number of people in the organization. That said, let's get back to our scenario. Q3 ends with another miss and panic sets in. The probability of achieving the total year budget is out the window. At this point, they bring in Finance and HR personnel to help determine the best way to reduce corresponding cost. In other words, work up a headcount reduction plan. If for no other reason, demonstrate the company takes commitment seriously, which will likely also result in a few executive heads to roll. However, the brunt of the impact will surely be felt by the individual contributors in the Sales and Pursuit organizations. Most likely, many of the very same people that were hired less than one year ago.

I painted a rather bleak picture to make a point, which, believe it or not, is true to life in many cases. Let's consider the same scenario again. Only this time, assume the desired outcome was achieved. In other words, the total year revenue goal was attained. If that were to actually happen, it's important to be mindful that revenue growth does not occur simply because an organization added Sales and Pursuit resources. First and foremost, the company needs to possess products and/or services customers actually need and want. Furthermore, sales growth initiatives typically need to be accompanied by aggressive marketing and promotion campaigns that entice customers to buy more products and/or services. It's the combination of all three (products/services, marketing, and sales) that produce success, not just adding Sales and Pursuit personnel. By the way, you can have the biggest and the best sales force, but without compelling products or solutions, your ability to increase revenue is limited at best. Conversely, you can have the best products or solutions, but without an adequate size sales force and capable salespeople, your revenue growth will likewise be limited.

Finally, let's discuss the value-based hiring decision that proved to be worthwhile. In this case, the hiring manager justified bringing on a specialty systems analyst for a one-time need. Specifically, we were experiencing recurring performance issues with a homegrown business application system, which was written in a relatively unpopular computer language by someone who had long left the company. The system problems resulted in employee productivity losses, which we estimated to be approximately $500K/year. Our choices were clear. Either live indefinitely with the inherent issues, or do something to fix the root problem. We decided on the latter course of action for obvious reasons. We brought in an external systems analyst with whom we signed a six-month agreement, which contained several time-based progress milestones. The contract was an hourly fee agreement, which we estimated would end up costing approximately $200K to fix the problem. If our estimate was correct, the cost of the project represented less than half of the annual productivity loss we were experiencing.

Fast forward six months, the project was deemed a resounding success, which of course we were delighted with the outcome. Incidentally, what often happens in these situations, the hiring manager is so impressed with these so called *miracle workers,* they are reluctant to release the resource when the one-time project is completed. Instead, they attempt to justify keeping the resource on board to address other needs, which some may prove worthwhile while others will almost certainly not. In some situations, the hiring manager may even attempt to justify converting the specialty resource to a permanent employee. For the record, we did neither. We released the resource once the original project was successfully completed.

The potential danger with hiring a specialty resource like the one described, a time may soon come when it's no longer economically justifiable to keep the resource on board. When that happens, you are suddenly confronted with another issue, namely, a potential termination decision. No matter how you look at these types of situations, it always comes down to the value proposition. If there is quantifiable on-going value to be realized, that is greater than the resource cost, keeping the individual around makes sense? On the other hand, if it turns out the individual is only occasionally needed, keeping her around beyond the original engagement, or hiring her as a permanent employee is simply not smart business.

Bottom line, from a risk standpoint, given the option of going with need-based versus quantified value-based hiring justification, the latter is almost always a safer bet. However, as pointed out in one of the examples above, utilizing value-based justification does not necessarily guarantee a favorable outcome. Incidentally, there will be situations in which quantifying projected return value is simply not possible, leaving you no choice but to go with a faith-based hiring decision. In those cases, in lieu of leveraging quantitative data, applying a reasonable amount of foresight, intuition, and common sense will always serve you better than simply going with blind faith. Furthermore, a post-hiring evaluation should always be done to determine whether or not a wise hiring decision was actually made.

Chapter 5

Direct Labor Resource Cost and Value Management

In MPS businesses, and for that matter essentially all Managed Services businesses, direct labor resources are generally categorized as being either dedicated or shared. Dedicated resources are tied to a particular contracted deal, which is generally assigned a unique cost center number to capture all deal related costs and produce a corresponding Deal P&L. Accounting doesn't get any easier and more straightforward. On the other hand, shared resource cost is more involved. Meaning, there are two steps required to get cost assigned to the appropriate deal cost center. The initial cost capture is straightforward. That is to say, all of the labor related cost for those resources is initially posted to a designated shared cost center. For example, transition manager costs are initially posted to the Transition Department cost center. The second step involves moving reported expended labor cost from the shared to the appropriate deal cost center. That's where a Labor Tracking & Costing system comes into play, something we will discuss in more detail shortly.

This is a good time to briefly digress and explain how shared cost centers differ from dedicated deal cost centers. Let's assume the MPS business is a separate BU within a large product company. That BU would most likely have three different types of cost centers: dedicated, shared, and management cost centers. Although not necessarily relevant to this discussion, it's worthwhile to briefly mention management cost centers in order to provide a complete picture. Those cost centers are used to collect expenses for the BU management team, as well as other admin and analytical functions within the business unit. Since all costs incurred by the BU have to be reflected in Deal P&Ls, expenses that are captured in management and other admin cost centers are allocated to Deal P&Ls. Although the allocation methodology may vary, the distributing of those expenses is typically based on the percentage of total revenue or cost each deal represents.

In an ideal situation, all expenses captured in shared cost centers would be liquidated each month. In other words, the cost center would be zeroed out. The way that happens, when shared resources charge their time (cost) to deal cost centers, the shared cost centers those resources are assigned receive the corresponding credit. This process is commonly referred to as *cost relief.* In a perfect world, every expense dollar that is posted to shared cost centers is liquidated each month via labor cross-charges. It's safe to say that is essentially never the case. The leftover or over-charged amount remaining in the shared cost center is referred to as *residual,* which is allocated to the Deal P&Ls each month end. Here again, although the allocation methodology may vary, it is commonly done using the same methodology as allocated management and admin expense. In other words, typically based on percentage of total revenue or cost. From my personal experience, I can safely say negative residual is far more common than positive residual. In which case, Deal P&Ls Owners receive an additional cost charge they are surely *not* happy, and often complain about the *unjustifiable* expense allocation. The fact of the matter, if you want to publish fully burdened Deal P&Ls, residual expense must somehow be reflected in those P&Ls.

Shared support is typically handled one of two ways. One way is having a resource provide 100% support to a particular deal for a defined period of time. For example, a transition manager working 100% of her time on a specific big deal for, let's say, one year. Incidentally, the difference between that transition manager and a full-time dedicated deal resource like a delivery manager, the latter would be 100% dedicated for the entire term of the deal. Whereas, the transition manager is involved only as long as it takes to complete the transition phase of the deal. Unlike full-time dedicated deal resources, these individuals move in and out of deals as needed. From an accounting standpoint, assigning cost to the deal that transition manager is supporting for one year is relatively easy because it's not time based. Instead, her salary and all other employee-related expenses for that one year are cross-charged in its entirety from the shared cost center she is assigned to the deal cost center she is supporting.

Now comes the more challenging and more common scenario that occurs most often in MPS and other Managed Services businesses. In this case, let's assume a transition manager is simultaneously supporting four relatively small deals. So, how do you assign transition cost to those four deal cost centers? A fast and easy way is to divide the total cost of the transition manager by four, and allocate equal amounts to each of the four deals. However, that approach is as imperfect as it is easy.

A more accurate way is to capture the actual amount of time worked on each of the four deals and assign the corresponding cost to the deal cost centers. The reason this approach is better, there are several factors that can influence the amount of actual time worked on each deal. For example, each deal could be in a different transition phase. Transition activity normally spikes mid-phase, whereas it gradually increases in the early phase and gradually decreases in the late phase. Another factor, depending on the transition duration and deal complexity, the amount of transition support each deal requires can vary. Therefore, the only fair and equitable way of charging shared transition cost to deals is by utilizing a Labor

Tracking & Costing system. These systems capture actual hours worked and corresponding cost, which is subsequently charged to each deal cost center.

We talked fairly extensively about the cost side of direct labor measurement and management. Now let's briefly discuss the value side. I'm going to keep this simple. In most cases, there is a correlation between the amount of direct labor expended and the amount of business volume generated, regardless of whether we're talking about product or service volume. Once you have established a baseline resource to volume ratio, it's easy to detect imbalances when it occurs. Generally speaking, when direct resource levels remain constant and business volumes are higher, that's a good thing from a value standpoint. Whereas, when direct resource levels remain constant and business volumes drop, that's a bad thing that needs to be rectified. On the other hand, when resources are being added, there is a presumption the resource to volume ratio will minimally remain the same. In which case, if you're adding 20% direct labor and achieving only 15% incremental volume, you would have an unfavorable situation. Whereas, if you're adding 20% direct labor and achieving 25% incremental volume, you would have a favorable situation. The fact of the matter, management will most likely expect the resource to volume ratio to improve with added resources. In other words, benefit from economies of scale.

Utilizing Labor Tracking & Costing Systems

In most MPS and other types of Managed Services (MS) businesses, Labor Tracking & Costing tools are commonly used to track and distribute shared resource labor cost to contracted Deal P&Ls. They are also used to measure, manage, and compare individual resource utilization to norms. There are several factors that influence the mix of shared versus dedicated resources in these businesses. Nevertheless, it's safe to say shared resources make up the majority of the direct labor pool in most of these businesses, which is precisely the reason using a Labor Tracking & Costing tool is critically important.

Theoretically, these tools can be as simple as manual spreadsheets, which can be used as source documents to manually post cost to the General Ledger (GL). Practically speaking, integrated application systems that have automated cost posting capability to the GL are more common and a great deal more useful. Furthermore, these systems generally have built-in standard and ad hoc reporting capability, which provide managers a means to efficiently identify problems and take quick corrective actions. Incidentally, a small MPS or other MS business might be able to get away with a spreadsheet solution. However, most moderate-size and large businesses could not operate effectively without an automated tool.

Now let's talk about fully burdened labor rates, which represent an integral component built into Labor Tracking & Costing tools. But before we do, a few words about what is a fully burdened labor rate. Simply put, these labor rates include hourly wage, plus fringe and other labor-related overhead, plus regional management overhead, plus a utilization factor. We'll discuss these elements in more detail shortly. Nevertheless, the reason labor rate accuracy is important, actual hours worked multiplied by the fully burdened labor rate is what's reflected in Deal P&Ls. In which case, labor charges to Deal P&Ls are only as good as the fully burdened labor rate assumptions. In other words, a moderate 5 - 10 % labor rate error could easily make the difference between a profitable versus unprofitable Deal P&L. Just so there is no misunderstanding, allow me to clarify one very important point before discussing this matter further. From a total company P&L standpoint, these labor rates do *not* matter. The reason being, burdened labor rates are strictly created and used to measure deal profitability. Furthermore, if you want to be able to identify which deals are profitable and which are not, it's important to have reasonably accurate burdened labor rates.

At this point you might be wondering, if you have an overall profitable business, why is having accurate burdened labor rates so important? Let me answer that question by posing another question. What savvy and profit-conscious business manager would not want to improve overall business profitability? If you're managing a large services deal portfolio, there is only one way to distinguish profitable from unprofitable deals. You must be able to produce individual Deal P&Ls to identify which deals are generating profit versus those that are eating your profit. Since shared labor charges typically make up a significant portion of the overall deal cost, applying inaccurate burdened labor rates will surely result in misleading Deal P&Ls. On the other hand, having accurate Deal P&Ls allows you to make informed decisions regarding individual deals in your portfolio. In some cases, that may mean making tough decisions. For example, cutting your losses by tactfully severing relationship with a client there is no hope of improving profitability.

Listen, I know it's more complicated than what I just described in the real world, especially with strategic accounts that do business with companies on multiple fronts, buying products and services from multiple BUs. Global and strategic accounts clearly need to be managed more holistically, meaning you have to accept the fact some deals with those clients may be profitable while others may not. Making matters even more complicated, some businesses have written or unwritten reciprocity agreements with one another. In those situations, you must be particularly careful not to make isolated decisions that could potentially have broader undesirable implications with those clients.

Let's get back to fully burdened labor rates and talk about how they are created. You start with average gross annual salary by job code. Let's assume the average salary for a particular job code is $80,000. To which you add 25% fringe plus 25% for other labor-related overhead, making the burdened gross salary $120,000. To that, let's add 12.5% regional management overhead, making the regionally burdened salary $135,000. As mentioned earlier, when creating fully burdened labor rates for Labor Tracking & Costing tools, there is one additional item that must be considered in the calculation, namely, a utilization factor. It's hardly reasonable to assume a service organization can realize 100% utilization from any given individual. In other words, achieve 100% productive time. The fact of the matter, there will be down time for admin work, training, vacation, sick time, as well as potential unproductive bench time that needs to be factored into the fully burdened labor rates. From my experience, I'd say a reasonable utilization assumption for a typical MPS or other MS business is somewhere between 85 - 90 %. For the following demonstrations, we will assume a 90% utilization factor.

To give you an appreciation for how fully burdened labor rates are created, let's work up a few examples. Assuming 52 weeks and a 40-hour work week, there are 2,080 available hours in a year. Starting with the regionally burdened salary expense of $135,000 (calculated above), gives us an hourly labor rate of $64.90 ($135,000 / 2,080 hours). When we factor in the 90% utilization assumption, it reduces the total year available hours from 2,080 to 1,872. Therefore, the fully burdened labor rate that is entered into the Labor Tracking & Costing tool would be $72.12 ($135,000 / 1,872 hours). Ideally, you would create several different labor rates, one for each job code. Within a particular job family, you might have three or more job codes. Let's assume the transition manager job family has three job codes, including one for junior level, another for standard level, and another for expert level. Let's assume further the annual regionally burdened salaries for those three job codes are $115,000, $135,000, and $155,000, respectively.

Taking into consideration the 90% utilization factor would make the junior labor rate $61.43 ($115,000 / 1,872); the standard labor rate $72.12 ($135,000 / 1,872); and the expert labor rate $82.80 ($155,000 / 1,872). That's the level of detail that needs to be entered into the Labor Tracking & Costing tool in order to produce accurate and reliable Deal P&Ls.

As you can see, we did not use actual employee salaries in our examples, which there is likely considerable variation from one employee to another in the same job code. Instead, for manageability reasons, we used the average salary for each job code. Granted, that approach does not produce 100% accurate results. However, for (pro-forma) Deal P&L reporting purposes it's sufficient, and certainly much less cumbersome than having to deal with each individual's actual salary. Some companies may take a slightly more or less granular approach creating fully burdened labor rates. Ultimately, as long as the guidelines and assumptions used are reasonable and consistent, the resulting Deal P&Ls should be sufficiently reliable for managing deal level profitability.

At this point, I'd like to add some comments from my own personal experience. When I first heard the Managed Services organization I was working at the time required across the board use of a Labor Tracking & Costing tool, I cringed and challenged the value add. At that time, I was managing a fairly large client specific organization of 300 plus technical professionals. These individuals were providing a broad range of IT infrastructure support, as well as e-mail and other collaboration tools support for a very large global company. Although this was a dedicated client specific support organization, we were responsible for supporting four separate deals for this global client, each having different deliverables. Accordingly, the team was separated into four distinct sub-teams.

For accounting purposes, we set up four separate cost centers, one for each deal. Individuals on each sub-team were directly coded to their respective deal cost center, which meant sub-team costs were conveniently collected in those four distinct cost centers. Hence, we were able to produce accurate Deal P&Ls without the use of a Labor Tracking & Costing tool. Having those 300 plus people report hours worked on the tool would have provided marginal benefit at best, specifically, more granular reporting regarding actual tasks performed. Granted, that information might have been somewhat useful for analytical purposes. However, in my opinion, it was not worth the required on-going individual reporting effort. Not to mention the prerequisite training and constant compliance monitoring that would have also been required. Ultimately, my team was given a waiver, principally because there was essentially nothing to be gained from a P&L reporting standpoint. As a matter of fact, eventually the entire Managed Services BU adopted the following rule. All dedicated resources whose salary and other employee-related expenses are coded directly to a deal cost center were no longer required to report their time on the Labor Tracking & Costing tool. Needless to say, I was very happy with that ruling, which dovetails very nicely with one of the central themes of this book. Namely, any and all worthwhile investments must produce value greater than its cost.

My attitude about the value of utilizing a Labor Tracking & Costing tool changed dramatically when my role changed from supporting one large client to managing a regional portfolio that included a significant number of small, medium, and large deals. Also noteworthy, more than half of my portfolio revenue was generated from small and medium deals that had virtually no dedicated resources assigned to them. Even the ADMs for those deals were shared resources. In which case, utilizing a Labor Tracking & Costing tool suddenly became critically important to me and my team of ADMs. The reason being, without the use of the tool, it would have been virtually impossible to produce P&Ls for the individual deals in my portfolio. Moreover, without Deal P&Ls it would have been impossible to distinguish good from bad performing deals, which would have been problematic to say the least.

The two biggest challenges organizations typically face implementing and effectively utilizing tools like Labor Tracking & Costing systems are training and reporting discipline. Let's start with training. It goes without saying, information that you retrieve from any database is only as good as the quality of the input. Therefore, ensuring you secure high quality reported data starts with a robust training program. However, training alone is not sufficient. You can't just have a subject matter expert deliver a training presentation to a large group of users and expect those users to completely understand what is required from them. I have seen this oversimplified approach used and fail virtually every time it is attempted.

When it comes to tools training, how it's done matters as much as the quality of the training material. I have found small cohesive group training works best. For example, if you're training ADMs on a tool, your best bet is to bring together all the ADMs that report to a single region manager, let's say the Northeast Regional Manager. There are two things about this approach that help contribute to success. First, the group is guaranteed to be small since most region managers typically have no more than a dozen ADMs reporting to them. Second, since the team of ADMs routinely work together and are presumed to be comfortable with one another, it increases the likelihood of a lively and interactive training experience.

Training for a fairly complex tool like a Labor Tracking & Costing system should not be done in its entirety in a single session. For professional training, I have found short individually focused sessions work much better than longer all-encompassing training. Therefore, the best approach might be something like the following. Start with a one-hour presentation regarding the tool intent and functionality, allowing sufficient time for trainee questions and comments. A week later, in a separate two-hour training session, talk about how data is collected and stored in the tool, with particular emphasis on user input requirements. Once again, allow sufficient time for questions and comments. A week after that, have a third and final two-hour training session regarding the tool standard and ad hoc reporting capability. This session should include a discussion on how to interpret reported data and leverage it for troubleshooting purposes and making better informed business decisions.

I could get into much more detail about the benefits of short versus long duration training. Suffice it to say, one of the most notable shortcomings of the latter is experiencing some level of trainee fatigue and boredom. Bottom line, with regard to professional training, short sessions almost always work better than long.

Now let's talk about the second challenge, namely reporting discipline. In other words, to what extent each resource is consistently and accurately reporting their labor activity in the tool. Reporting discipline can be effectively managed with the compliance reporting functionality that is commonly available in Labor Tracking & Costing tools. For example, a Transition Department Manager can pull weekly reports showing the amount of labor activity reported by each of her team members. Ideally, you would want to see 100% compliance, meaning 40 hours reported for a normal workweek. With compliance reports, you can quickly and easily identify individuals who are reporting below an acceptable level. In which case, explanations for non-compliance would obviously be required, followed by a commitment to improve future reporting discipline.

On the other hand, if a manager has some individuals on her team who are reporting, let's say, 125 - 150% of normal work hours, those situations also require attention for different reasons. If these are non-exempt employees (in other words paid hourly), the organization would be incurring overtime expense for the extra hours worked. If that occurs occasionally, there is no need for concern. Paying overtime premium for intermittent labor spikes is reasonable and, in most cases, cost effective. On the other hand, if the overtime is relatively constant, managers would most likely be better off adding resources to the team who would be paid normal wages instead of incurring overtime premium expense.

If employees reporting excess hours are exempt, in other words paid a fixed salary, and not ordinarily compensated for overtime, managers should have other concerns. Generally speaking, except in unusual circumstances like a down economy, most salary employees will tolerate a reasonable amount of unpaid overtime, but only up to a point. Once that reasonableness threshold has been crossed, many of those employees will likely start looking for another job. Especially in situations that are not expected to improve anytime soon. Of course, depending on varying circumstances and personal reasons, everyone's threshold may be different. Nevertheless, managers need to be mindful those thresholds do exist, and be especially careful not to cross them. Otherwise, they run the risk of losing some of those employees. Furthermore, as most experienced people managers know, it's usually the better quality and highly sought-after employees that will leave first. Bottom line, managers who believe they can continuously take advantage of their employees need to realize there will eventually be consequences resulting from that shortsighted management approach.

Let's continue our discussion regarding reporting discipline a while longer. If you are striving to achieve a certain behavior from professional employees in your organization, first and foremost you must have management support. Without that, your attempt to affect behavior is almost guaranteed to fail and result in a total waste of time and effort. To demonstrate the importance of management support or lack thereof, allow me share a relatively recent personal experience.

One of my recent assignments was working on a Business Analysis team. We were responsible for reviewing and analyzing BU business activity and accompanying financials, with a constant eye on profit improvement opportunities. Our team worked very closely with Business Finance. As a matter of fact, the two teams were so integrated that some people mistakenly thought we were Finance resources. Both teams supported the Americas Region, meaning we were responsible for overseeing activities in the USA, Canada, and Latin America sub-regions.

With regard to Deal P&L integrity, there were significant differences across the region. Among other contributing factors, the principal difference was the three sub-regions handled shared resource labor tracking and costing differently. Only the USA sub-region had long been utilizing a Labor Tracking & Costing tool. Canada had just started implementing the tool. Therefore, from a Deal P&L integrity standpoint, they still had lots of catching up to do. None of the Latin American countries were utilizing a Labor Tracking & Costing tool, which basically meant they were unable to produce reliable Deal P&Ls. In addition, there were inconsistencies and questionable accounting practices occurring in various countries across the Latin American sub-region, which also contributed to their inability to produce reliable Deal P&Ls. Suffice it to say, without accurate accounting for shared labor cost, compounded by questionable accounting practices, there was essentially no way of knowing which Latin American deals were profitable and which were not. Whereupon, we concluded there were some significant problems that needed to be addressed in order to remedy the situation.

First and foremost, we embarked on an educational exercise to convince the local country managers why a Labor Tracking & Costing tool was essential to accurately determining deal profitability. Second, we addressed the accounting inconsistencies with the Country and Region Finance organizations, which were rectified within a few short months. On the other hand, the journey to address the labor tracking and costing issue took the better part of two years before the tool was finally implemented in all of the Latin American countries. After the tool was implemented, we had the non-enviable task of training all the local resources how to use the tool. Given the different spoken languages (Spanish and Portuguese) and the different country cultures, it would be an understatement to say this was a challenging undertaking. In retrospect, the one thing I can say with absolute certainty is that without local management support we would still be trying to get users to utilize the tool. The underlying point of this story is that it's virtually impossible to affect resource behavior without management support. Try if you will, but you will most likely fail without that essential element of support.

Maximizing Direct Labor Resource Value

Direct labor resources represent the engine that runs most businesses. Without them, products are not manufactured, software and solutions are not created, and customers are not serviced and supported. Assuming resources are well placed and trained, there is typically a correlation between the number of direct labor resources and output volume. When we talk about managing the impact direct labor has on the P&L, we're really talking about ways to maximize resource utilization with such things as: standardizing, training and development, streamlining business processes, and more.

Furthermore, improving utilization starts with understanding where you are today and where you will want to be in the future. In MPS and other MS businesses, that makes leveraging a Labor Tracking & Costing tool absolutely essential. Otherwise, it's all guesswork, and you will not know whether you are under or over-utilizing your direct labor resources. Moreover, if not managed properly, both under and over-utilization can be consequential (more on this in a moment).

Once you have established a utilization baseline of let's say 85%, you can then start drilling down into reported labor and cost details to look for improvement opportunities. In other words, look for ways to get direct labor utilization closer to 90%. For example, you might notice significant utilization variations amongst like individuals, let's say transition managers. The variations may be due to issues and challenges with specific individuals, or extenuating circumstances that may exist with specific contracted deals those individuals are supporting. In either case, the reports provide a starting point for the analysis, which will eventually lead to implementing required corrective actions.

Incidentally, when underutilization occurs, there is always reason for concern and need to implement corrective actions. On the other hand, although overutilization is generally viewed as something positive, that is not always the case. As mentioned earlier, constant or excessive overutilization is almost guaranteed to have adverse ramifications. Meaning, either incurring unnecessary overtime cost for hourly wage employees, or increasing the risk of losing valued salaried employees who are not compensated for overtime. Next, I'd like to discuss the impact some common tools have on maximizing direct labor utilization, starting with standardizing.

Standardization

In virtually all businesses, including both product and service businesses, standardization is a powerful means of maximizing resource utilization. Generally speaking, the more a company standardizes, the lower will be the cost of manufacturing products or delivering services, which ultimately results in better ability to compete. If your competitors are leveraging standardized methods and processes and your company is not, it's virtually impossible for your company to compete on the basis of cost and price. Let's face it, in the marketplace price is king, which is especially true as products and service become increasingly commoditized.

As with most personal decisions one contemplates, business decisions must consider all of the related pros and cons before a final decision is made. Making standardization decisions in service businesses are no different. One of the pros that will likely be given maximum consideration is lowering operating cost. However, the flip side of lowering operating cost is potentially adversely impacting customer satisfaction. Service organizations must always be mindful of the impact standardization might have on their clients. The obvious reason, some customers may not be happy with how they are affected by standardization. Therefore, some extra effort may be required to smooth things over with some clients *beforehand,* not after you have already implemented standardized processes.

For example, an MPS or other MS business might decide to reorganize Technical Support from a client specific support structure to a centralized structure that handles all clients. From a call management standpoint, a centralized structure would almost certainly be more efficient and better suited to handle call volume fluctuations, in particular call spikes. Although that may be beneficial for the MSP organization from a process efficiency and cost effectiveness standpoint, customers may not like the impact that change has on them. The reason being, they may have grown accustomed and comfortable talking with a handful of client dedicated technicians, and had a sense those technicians understood their unique business needs. Being funneled into a general pool of technical support technicians will certainly not give them the same sense of being a *special client.*

Obviously, this type of change can backfire on the MSP organization if not handled with extraordinary care. In particular, establishing a reasonable level of comfort with affected clients beforehand. It may even require some sort of compromise, or a good faith reciprocity gesture on the part of MSP. The example I just shared represents only one of numerous potential impacts that could result from standardization. I simply wanted to convey that there is a multitude of factors that have to be considered when making a standardization decision. The obvious reason, it's not just the impact on the company's business processes and financial performance that matter. More importantly is the impact on the client and their willingness to accept the standardized change.

Now let's look at an example where standardized processes exist; however, a new contract that is being sold contains non-standard support requirements. Speaking from personal experience, I can tell you this is something MSPs commonly face. At any rate, let's assume you have a team of 500 delivery resources who are responsible for supporting an MPS deal portfolio. And, to a large extent, your team leverages standardized processes. Wouldn't it be nice if it stayed that way for the foreseeable future? Sure it would, but here's the thing. When new deals are being sold, customers will often request non-standard deliverables which your existing delivery processes cannot accommodate without modifications. As challenging as that may be for the Delivery organization, Sales is typically only interested in one thing, selling the deal (deliverable or not).

Although delivery personnel are often involved in the deal solution process, any push-back on their part is usually met with considerable pressure to back off and allow the deal to move forward as requested by the client. It's not hard to guess what happens next. The deal is signed and the non-standard deliverables move from being a contract negotiation challenge for Sales to a long-term deliverables challenge for Delivery. As difficult as it may be, the delivery organization will eventually find ways to make the one-off solutions work, which could take several months to implement and stabilize. Unfortunately, lurking behind one challenge will typically be another one-off challenge that Delivery will soon be facing. Bottom line, this is a seemingly endless vicious cycle, in which the delivery organization is essentially always left holding the bag (so to speak).

By the way, if the delivery organization cannot figure out how to address the one-off challenge, they will be viewed as the *bad guys.* Meanwhile, the Sales and Solution team get to walk away with their incentive compensation shortly after the deal is signed. Some companies are getting smarter by withholding portions of the Sales incentive by tying it to the first few years of Deal P&L performance, which is definitely a step in the right direction. Bottom line, if the company is not making money on the deal, neither should the Sales and Solution team receive 100% of their incentive compensation. Especially when they are selling hard to deliver and/or non-profitable deals.

So, how do you address this problem? One way is to ask the Sales Team to work harder at selling standard deliverables. Yes, there are times when customers can be unreasonably demanding. However, it's amazing how flexible many of those customers become, when you make it interesting for them with, let's say, a lower price. The point being, standardization is clearly a good thing from a resource utilization standpoint. And, as long as the Sales and Solution team is willing to work with the client to keep deliverables as standard as possible, it can be a win/win/win solution. Meaning, it helps the Delivery organization lower cost; provides the customer a more competitive price; and increases the probability the Sales and Solution team will sell the deal and earn their incentive compensation.

I'd like to make one final point regarding additional benefits derived from standardizing service delivery. Standardized delivery models inherently offer more opportunity to segment and potentially move portions of the support to lower cost locations. The opposite is true when organizations are required to support several non-standard deliverables, which are inherently more costly and cumbersome. And yes, my reference to lower cost locations could very well mean offshoring some of the work. Lower cost can also mean moving some support to a less costly part of the nation. Incidentally, my comment should not be construed as a blind endorsement for offshoring because it's not. I will tell you from personal experience, effective offshoring does not come easy and it does not always work as intended. Typically, there are several challenges that have to be overcome implementing a successful offshore solution. Nevertheless, sometimes you simply have no choice but to offshore. The reason being, if your competition is taking advantage of low-cost offshore support and you are not, your ability to compete will almost certainly be adversely impacted.

Training and Development

Another thing that can improve direct labor resource utilization is training initiatives. Although typically done with the best intentions, training initiatives often turn out to be ineffective. Why you might ask? Because how training is created and delivered matters as much as the content itself. First and foremost, failed initiatives often lack involvement by people from the organization being trained. Generally speaking, trainees are more likely to embrace training that is created and delivered by someone within their own organization. Whereas, training that is created and delivered by *outsiders* is almost never received with the same level of interest and enthusiasm. Throughout my career I have participated in the development and rollout of several training initiatives. By far, initiatives that involved people from the organization being trained proved more effective and successful.

Allow me to share an example of a recent personal experience. We assembled a team to develop and deliver P&L improvement training to a national team of Account Delivery Mangers (ADMs). The training involved two separate segments. The first segment covered a basic understanding of P&L management, which was delivered by a credible and well-respected finance manager. This individual was able to take a relatively complicated subject and break it down to simple, straightforward language, while utilizing several examples to help solidify trainee understanding. The feedback we received from this segment of the training was overwhelmingly positive.

The second segment, which was delivered by an individual from the delivery management community, focused on how to effectively leverage available levers and knobs to improve contracted deal profitability. From past failed experience, we thought it would be best to have the training delivered by someone within the trainee community, instead of an outsider such as a finance or business analyst. Just as with the first training segment, success versus failure came down to one word, credibility. In the latter case, who more credible than someone who has lived the experience to talk about how to successfully leverage available levers and knobs? If the same exact training material had been delivered by a finance or business analyst, I can almost guarantee we would not have achieved the same positive results. Why? Because, as most of us know from our own experiences, the person telling the story (delivering the training) matters as much as the story itself (the training material).

In addition to who and how training is most effectively delivered, there are a few training best practices I would like to discuss, starting with the importance of pre-requisite foundational knowledge. You can have the best training material possible and still fail miserably with your rollout. One of the principal reasons, the people you are training do not possess sufficient pre-requisite foundational knowledge. For example, you cannot effectively deliver P&L management training to a group of people who do not at least possess fundamental financial knowledge. Just as you cannot effectively deliver technical training to a group of people who do not possess fundamental product knowledge.

Throughout my career, I've seen this simple-minded approach attempted and fail several times. We are not talking about the trainees' intellectual capacity here. Instead, we're talking about the fact that most training is progressive and works like building blocks, with one layer added on top of another. My point being, when you launch a training initiative, make sure the training will be delivered to people who possess the necessary foundational knowledge. Otherwise, the rollout of your training initiative is almost guaranteed to fail.

Next, I'd like to talk about two important aspects of training that could very well make the difference between success and failure. The first is regarding delivery method, and the second is regarding the training audience size and make-up. I'd like to start by stating, dialog will always produce better results than monolog. Regardless of who you place in front of the trainees, if that person is robotically walking through a PowerPoint presentation, the training will most likely result in failure. On the other hand, utilizing a trainer that can effectively engage the audience and encourage dialog amongst the trainees will most likely result in success. No one likes to be talked to. If you want people to really listen and learn, you must find a way to engage them in the conversation.

In order to start the conversation, the trainer must first find a way to break the ice with the trainees. So, what's the best way to do that? Know your audience. Encourage one or more people in the audience who you know to get the conversation started with questions or comments. It never ceases to amaze me, when one individual starts, others will invariably follow. And before you know it, you have much of the training audience contributing to a robust training event. What better way to get the juices flowing? Dialog is contagious! Getting started is the only hard part. So, when you're deciding on the best person to deliver the training, don't make the common mistake of selecting the person who possesses the most subject matter knowledge. If that person cannot relate to the trainees, and is unable to get them involved in a conversation, you chose the wrong person. Instead, settle on someone with less knowledge if you have to, as long as she possesses the necessary people skills to make the training experience engaging and successful.

Now let's move on to the importance of training audience size and make-up. Typically, there are several factors that go into training decisions, which some will be influenced by economic considerations. Audience size is clearly one factor that has economic implications. I believe it's fair to say, the smaller the training audience, generally the better the training results. For example, it would be difficult for anyone to argue that 1:1 training produces the best results. The reason being, the trainer who is conveying the knowledge can instantly see whether or not the information is acknowledged and understood by the trainee. In which case, if deemed necessary, the trainer can quickly react with changes to the delivery approach. But, here is the problem with 1:1 training. It's very expensive!

The next best thing from both an economic and results standpoint is small group training of, let's say, 1 trainer to roughly 10 trainees. Although there are limited places for trainees to hide (so to speak) in these situations, there is no guarantee the training material will be absorbed by everyone. On the other hand, small group training is not nearly as expensive as 1:1 training. Next, let's assume a group of 50 individuals are being trained. Undoubtedly, from a cost perspective, that would be the most economical approach. However, it's virtually guaranteed some trainees will walk out of the training session with little or no more knowledge than when they walked into the training.

Like most business decisions, optimal training group size comes down to tradeoff value. For example, if you're doing general product knowledge training for a team of salespeople, a 1 to 50 approach may be perfectly acceptable. After all, salespeople are typically not expected to be product knowledge specialists. So, if they miss some of the training points, no big deal. On the other hand, if you're training 50 technicians on knowledge they will require to service and support new product, it is a big deal if some of those technicians walk out of the training clueless. In that case, a 1 to 10 training approach might be more suitable. Bottom line, training group size matters from both an affectivity and economic standpoint. Furthermore, a well-trained workforce, particularly in service businesses, is one of the principal keys to success.

The make-up of a training audience is also important. Unlike a classic academic environment, in which case diversity typically enhances the educational experience, the opposite is generally true in a corporate training environment. A good example of the former is a classroom of experienced professionals participating in an MBA program. The diversity and real-life experiences each student brings to the class and shares with classmates will undoubtedly enrich the educational experience. On the other hand, I found homogeneity to be more important than diversity in a corporate training environment. The reason being, like professionals typically relate better and are more comfortable with one another. Furthermore, people in large mixed training audiences are often reluctant to ask questions or make comments, fearing they may sound stupid. Whereas, those same fears/concerns are generally not nearly as evident when like professionals are being trained. Incidentally, if you want to see trainees at their best, have their manager participate in the training session. It's amazing how much more attentive and alive people tend to be when the person responsible for their performance review is in the same room.

At this point, I'd like to share a related personal experience. One of the most successful training series I ever participated was delivering operations and finance management training to several individual teams of ADMs. Members of each team reported to 1 of 5 regional portfolio managers. Furthermore, the individuals on each team were very comfortable with one another since they regularly met to discuss routine business matters with their manager. Moreover, they all had common problems and challenges. So, they naturally related well to one another. The great thing about these training events, one individual would ask a question or make a comment, which would quickly be followed by another person engaging in the conversation. The best way to describe what occurred, it was contagious in a good way. The resulting dialog was encouraging, and the training experience was successful. I am confident, if you were to ask the individual participants about both the experience and the outcome, the overwhelming majority would agree with my assessment.

For economic or other business reasons, let's assume you have no choice but to deliver training to a large group of diversified professionals who routinely work with one another. This is precisely what happened at a recent National Sales and Services Kick-off Meeting training event. If you're not familiar with these annual kick-off meetings, I will tell you they are very expensive. And, they take numerous people away from their day-to-day job responsibilities for the better part of a week. Thus, management will do everything reasonably possible to make the best use of allotted time, including having larger than ideal focused training sessions.

In the focused training session I am about to describe, there were approximately 75 ADMs plus 25 people from various support functions like Finance and Business Operations. The subject matter was best practices Deal P&L management, which we were allotted three hours for the training event. I realize that sounds like a lot of time for a breakout training event. Given the broad and complex subject matter, that was the minimum amount of time we required. So, here is what we did to make the best use of the allotted time. Before starting the training session, we told the trainees that at the end of the presentation segment we would assemble breakout teams to work through a related business scenario. That pre-training announcement encouraged most attendees to pay closer attention than they might otherwise have. It worked much like your teacher in high school or professor in college saying "pay special attention to the following because it will be on the test." In our situation, I am quite sure the motivating factor was, no one wanted to appear clueless in front of their peers during the breakout session.

As promised, when the presentation segment was completed, we assembled ten breakout teams with approximately ten people on each team. We provided each team the same written business scenario along with additional complementary material, and instructed them they had one hour to solve the problem. Also, we told them each team had to select a spokesperson who would be given ten minutes to present the team's findings. The interactions that occurred during the group breakouts were lively and interesting. Furthermore, the discussion that occurred when the team findings were presented to the entire training audience was a magnificent thing to watch. Best of all, it was remarkable to see the whole room come alive with constructive and healthy dialog. In retrospect, I'd have to say this training event proved to be as close to ideal as possible. By the way, after the participants completed the feedback evaluation for the entire kick-off meeting, this event received the best overall breakout training rating. The lesson learned, with a little ingenuity and foresight, you can turn a challenging situation like this large mixed group training event into successful outcome.

Although it may not be obvious to everyone, mentoring is an ideal complement to professional training and development. I will explain the reason in a moment. Most professional organizations consist of individuals that possess varying levels of knowledge and experience, ranging from novice to expert level. Furthermore, it's important to be mindful, training is typically not a one-time event. Moreover, training alone can only go so far to help produce valuable and knowledgeable resources. It must be coupled with experience, which can come from a couple of different sources, one's own experience and/or mentor shared experience. Regarding the latter, assigning an expert level mentor to guide and assist a novice professional can both enhance and expedite the learning and development process.

Alternatively, it's certainly possible for individuals to strictly learn from their own experiences, but that approach will definitely be a slower and longer path to follow. Progressive training coupled with mentoring is unquestionably the shorter and more expeditious path. Sure, mentoring can take some otherwise productive time away from the expert level resource.

However, in most cases, the payback to the organization makes mentoring a worthwhile investment.

Finally, I'd like to add, as important as training and development is to success, one must be mindful of its limitations. Let me give you a vivid example of what I am referring. I was personally involved in a long-term training initiative to convert approximately 100 ADMs to P&L managers. As subtle as that may sound, it wasn't. There is a huge difference between simply managing a customer account and being held accountable for profit contribution. Most of the people I am referring were initially hired as operations managers. Meaning they were responsible for delivering contracted services and achieving stated levels of customer satisfaction. However, they were not held accountable for the P&L performance of their respective contracted deal. It's important to point out that several of these individuals possessed absolutely no prior P&L management experience. The fact of the matter, they did not have to because that was not part of the original job requirement. Therein lies the biggest challenge we faced, which I will explain in a moment.

Although the organization previously produced Deal P&Ls, they were virtually useless. The reason being, those P&Ls were generated by a small team of offshore financial resources that were inexperienced and were not properly trained. Bottom line, there were several significant cost omissions in the P&Ls, which created the illusion that most of the deals were very profitable. Once we straightened out the accounting issues and started producing accurate and reliable Deal P&Ls, management suddenly realized several of our contracted deals were actually in financial trouble. Shortly thereafter, the ADM training initiative I referred to earlier was launched. Incidentally, the previous P&Ls were so outrageously misstated that if a deal did not reflect 50% or greater gross margin it was considered a loser. The fact of the matter, not only were essentially all of the deals not producing anywhere near 50% gross margin, several were actually under water. In other words, generating negative gross margin.

Let's get back to the P&L management training initiative. After more than one year of progressive P&L training, we failed to realize the lofty goal we set for ourselves, namely, converting 100% of the operations managers to P&L managers. To be clear, this was sporadic training that occurred throughout the year, which was equivalent to approximately four weeks of training. In the final analysis, we actually realized approximately 75% of our goal. In which case, 25% of the ADMs proved to be proficient at managing Deal P&Ls, and another 50% absorbed sufficient knowledge to adequately manage P&Ls. The remaining 25% were still in various stages of cluelessness regarding P&L management. Why you might be wondering? Some people, as good as they were operations managers, were unable to make the connection between business activities and the financials. Simply put, grasping financial concepts was simply not in their DNA, which meant there was no way we would achieve 100% of our goal, even with additional training.

Instead, we were faced with the hard reality that several of those ADMs needed to be replaced with people who possessed newly required skills. I realize it's not fair that someone would be displaced for an after the fact job requirement. Welcome to the ever-challenging and sometimes very unfair world of business! The lesson learned, you can invest all you want in training and development, but in some cases, it will simply not produce desired results. The reason being, if the people you are training do not possess the aptitude, desire, and/or willingness to learn because they are suddenly out of their comfort zone, you are basically wasting time and money training those individuals.

Streamlining Business Processes

Finally, let's talk about maximizing direct labor resource utilization by streamlining and/or improving business processes. Once you have honed in on a problematic and/or antiquated business process, the first thing you need to do is flowchart the existing process. If a flowchart already exists, make sure it's accurate and up to date. If a flowchart does not exist, create one. In either case, be sure to involve subject matter experts in this important first step, as well as all of the subsequent process rebuilding steps.

Some companies do a good job keeping their business processes up to date. Other companies do the complete opposite, from having no documentation to having neglected or outdated process documentation. When one of the latter conditions exists, business processes are only as good as the quality and accuracy of verbal information that is passed down from one employee to the next, which is really a dangerous way to run a business. That is particularly true in situations there is significant employee attrition. Even worse, are situations in which a key employee, who mentally possesses undocumented business processes, never shows up for work again for some reason or another. If and when that happens, you will undoubtedly experience unpleasant consequences, as well as have a significant time-consuming challenge on your hands. Meaning, you will have to document those processes starting with a blank sheet of paper.

For the most part, business processes become outdated or obsolete when one of the following events occurs: introduction of new business system or tool, acquisition, divestiture, and any number of other significant changes that may occur in a company. As these fast-moving and challenging activities occur, one of the last things busy people think about is updating business process documents. That is, until they are faced with the consequences of having outdated documentation. Ideally, organizations should routinely review their business process documents, and update them whenever a significant change occurs in the business. There is no such thing as everlasting business processes. As changes occur in a business, so too must those changes be reflected in updated process documents. The reason being, how business gets done will often influence resource utilization, which will ultimately influence business profitability.

Chapter 6

Indirect Labor Resource Cost and Value Management

I'd like to start this chapter by stating the obvious. Most companies cannot successfully operate without a reasonable number of indirect or overhead resources. That said, the fundamental challenge companies face is ensuring the return value of indirect labor resources outweigh their cost. Just as with direct labor, obtaining indirect labor cost is relatively straightforward. It's simply a matter of capturing salary plus fringe and all other employee-related expenses for those individuals. However, capturing indirect labor value is considerably more difficult and less precise than direct labor value. The primary reason, there is less correlation between indirect resources and business volume as there is with direct resources. Therefore, determining the value of indirect resources must oftentimes be based on the basis of either reported changes in related performance indicators or reasonable correlating assumptions.

Let's briefly consider one category of overhead resources, namely, management. Unless you're running a small mom and pop operation, most companies require a reasonable amount of management leadership. Without management, companies would lack the vision and direction required to successfully run the business. Furthermore, as companies grow in size and complexity, they normally require specialty resources in the following overhead functions. Finance to manage the accounting and financial analysis. Human Resources to manage the workforce. Legal to provide legal protection and risk management. And, any number of other administrative and support functions required to effectively run the business. Therefore, the question regarding overhead resources is not whether they are required or not. It's a question of how many are truly necessary and justifiable on the basis of cost versus return value. Unfortunately, many companies do not make indirect resource hiring decisions with payback value in mind. That is one of the primary reasons so many companies end up with too many indirect resources, which, in many cases, do nothing more than burden the business with unnecessary cost.

Indirect Resources Have Varying Impact on Profitability

Indirect resources tend to either be project oriented or part of general overhead. Although a reasonable number of general overhead resources are essential to run most businesses, overhead functions are often overstaffed. In which case, the value of some of those resources is questionable at best. On the other hand, the value of project oriented indirect resources is more easily identified and, in most cases, worthwhile with the following condition. Those resources must be released or re-assigned when the project they are hired to do is completed. Keeping them around to handle non-critical projects, or just in case they may be needed in the future, is simply not smart business.

At this point, I'd like to share a couple of real-life examples of newly assigned indirect resources, which one proved worthwhile and the other did not. The worthwhile example involved moving an existing indirect resource into a newly created long-term project. This particular individual was sought after because he possessed extensive business knowledge and experience, as well as extraordinary data mining skills, which both were required to successfully tackle this project. Actually, this individual was relentless when it came to data mining. Anecdotally, we referred to him as the data maniac. The project he was tasked involved a runaway problem with embedded lease write-offs, which amounted to $3-4M per year. If you're familiar with embedded leases that are associated with contracted services, great. If you're not, it's not terribly important to the underlining point I am trying to make. Suffice to say, this problem was absolutely eating away at what could have otherwise been profit for this relatively new business unit, which incidentally had not yet contributed any profit to the business.

It took several months of concentrated effort from this particular individual, plus lots of support from a cross-functional team to achieve initial success, which meant stopping the problem from growing further. After several more months of collaborative effort, we started to see a reversal in the trend. In other words, old long-standing issues were rapidly being resolved. Fast forwarding a couple years, the ongoing monthly embedded lease variance was essentially brought down to zero, and remained at roughly zero for several years that followed. To say the least, this was a remarkable accomplishment, which saved the company tens of millions of dollars. It was done with the right expert resource leading the effort, along with a great deal of support and perseverance from a cross-functional team that systematically chipped away at old lingering problems. Furthermore, outdated business processes, which were contributing to the problem, were updated to prevent similar issues from occurring in the future.

With regard to return value, there was no clear and concise way of establishing the actual value this particular individual brought back to the organization. Although, we do know losses were running at $3-4M per year before the problem was confronted head on. If we take a very conservative approach and consider just two years savings, we avoided $6-

8M embedded lease write-offs. Comparing that to this individual's fully burdened cost, plus the cost of ½ dozen or so part-time resources who assisted with the project during the two years, brings the total cost to less than $1M. Therefore, conservatively speaking, this project saved the company a minimum of $5M after expenses. Not bad, when you consider the fact this one indirect resource was principally responsible for this incredible turnaround.

Along these lines, I'd like to make one additional comment regarding new BUs. Generally speaking, the focus of a new BU is more on marketing and growing the business, and less on business controls and processes. That is precisely the reason focused sweeps like the one just described are particularly important for the long-term vitality and profitability of the new BU. Of course, focused sweeps are also useful in well-established businesses. The difference being, in well-established businesses, you generally have to look harder and deeper to find significant profit improvement opportunities. The reason being, the low hanging fruit (so to speak) will have likely already been picked.

The non-worthwhile example involved moving an existing people manager into a newly created individual contributor role, reporting to the same senior manager he reported to previously. The need for this position was the result of a recent Service organization realignment, which closely mirrored the reorganized Sales organization. Fundamentally, the move made sense since the two organizations worked very closely together and typically shared the same regional customers. The former manager I am referring volunteered for the individual contributor position principally because he had grown tired of dealing with people management issues, and particularly tired dealing with demanding and unreasonable clients. Dealing with seemingly never-ending people management issues and challenging clients can certainly contribute to management fatigue. Most ambitious individual contributors work hard to become people managers or client managers. Therefore, it's difficult for most people to understand and appreciate why someone would want to move backward into an individual contributor role. Believe me, it happens. Furthermore, when management fatigue sets in, affected managers want nothing more than to move out of their existing role, the sooner the better.

The fact of the matter, managing challenging organizations and/or clients can eventually take the wind out of your sails (so to speak). I've seen that very thing happen to several good managers who simply couldn't take it anymore. They desperately needed to get back to a more suitable situation in which they only needed to be concerned with self-management. Anyway, this particular individual ended up in a role coordinating a fairly significant regional realignment of customer accounts and widespread manager reporting changes. Without question, this was a critical one-time project that took approximately six months to complete. At that point, instead of moving this individual to an equally critical role, his manager kept him in that staff position to handle routine operations management matters. We already had a Business Operations organization in the BU that handled routine administrative matters. Therefore, there was no need for the costly redundancy.

Once again, we come back to the cost versus value principle. The cost of keeping this individual in that role beyond the initial six-month project was surely greater than the incremental value he subsequently brought back to the BU. How do I know that? I witnessed it with my own eyes. The tasks this individual worked on after the initial six-month project was completed could have easily and effectively been handled by a less experienced person on the Business Operations team. By the way, I am not suggesting that a proven employee with a good track record, such as this particular individual, should simply be discarded from the company when there is no apparent immediate need for his services. However, I am suggesting management needs to do a better job assigning these individuals where they are truly needed to make meaningful contributions, even if that means having to move the person around a few times before he finally settles into a worthwhile permanent position. Sure, it's a little more work on the manager's part. But in the long run, both the employee and the company will benefit from the manager's extra effort. Besides, it's the right thing to do.

From a profit contribution standpoint, the first example I shared represents more so the exception than the rule. Realistically speaking, I'd have to say most indirect resources have limited impact on profitability. If you believe the aggregate gazillion dollars saved by indirect resources, as reflected in their resumes, it would certainly add up to be more than enough money needed to cure world hunger (sarcasm). The fact of the matter, there is a significant amount of double counting and miscounting reflected in those grossly exaggerated claims. So, what is real? In most cases, it's hard to pinpoint. But one thing is for sure, it's nowhere near the exaggerated claims commonly made by indirect resources.

Let me give you an example of an exaggerated claim. Let's assume a Managed Print Services BU is struggling managing company owned toner inventory that is located at customer sites. Therefore, management decides to bring in a business analyst to scrutinize the details and develop a cost-effective solution that does not adversely affect customer satisfaction. After analyzing the situation for a couple of months, the analyst comes up with a viable solution that involves bringing back in house most of the inventory currently dispersed across multiple customer sites. Management agrees to implement the recommended solution, which is the first step of a fairly involved project to be undertaken.

Thereafter, the implementation phase, is when the real work gets done, which involves numerous people on the ground to execute the project plan. When the project is completed, let's say the team is able to successfully pull back $10M of inventory. So, what do you think is the savings amount reflected in the business analyst resume? You guessed it! He claims the entire $10M inventory reduction as a cost savings initiative that he led. Needless to say, that is a significant misrepresentation of the real value he was personally responsible for bringing back to the company for the following reasons. First, although the analysts should be credited for coming up with the solution, without help from people on the ground, none of the savings would have been realized. Second, counting the full value of the inventory removed from customer sites as savings is fundamentally flawed. Why you might ask? From a savings standpoint, if you assume the company needs to carry less inventory because it is centralized, the only legitimate value that can be claimed is a reduction in inventory carrying cost. Let's be conservative and say inventory carrying cost represents 20% of the inventory value. That means the real savings generated from this project would have been $2M. And, that's giving the analyst full credit, which would not have been possible without help from people on the ground.

That is one of numerous examples I could have shared regarding overstated and/or double counted credit claims that commonly occur with indirect resources. These individuals are most likely trying to justify their existence, or deliberately overstating their accomplishments to make their resume look good. Although the example I shared could be construed as shining a negative light on all indirect resources, it's not. Throughout my career, I have worked very closely with numerous indirect resources who have proven to be invaluable to the organizations they support. My simple point, without help and cooperation from others, indirect resources alone will generally have limited impact on the business bottom line.

Indirect Resources Tend to Creep Up in Organizations

If not watched and managed carefully, indirect resources tend to creep up in organizations beyond levels truly needed and justifiable. There is always a so-called *good reason* for adding another indirect resource to count, control, or analyze business activity. And, before you know it, you have a lopsided situation; whereby, indirect labor cost represents an ever-growing percentage of total labor cost. Although that situation should not be allowed to occur, those of us who have been in business for any length of time have witnessed otherwise. Nevertheless, when it's obvious an imbalance exists, management should take corrective action. Remember, cost is cost no matter where it originates. Furthermore, viable companies can only carry so much indirect labor cost before it starts to negatively impact profitability and their ability to compete.

Allow me to share a real-life example of indirect resource creep, which has to do with extraordinary Finance resource growth in an MPS business unit I recently worked. When I joined the BU, it had only existed for a couple of years and was generating approximately $50M in annual revenue. Relative to the entire company size, this was a small and insignificant business unit, which senior management was apparently convinced would eventually turn into a worthwhile investment. Just as with most new BUs, we were given some leeway and allowed to operate below break-even during the first few years. At that time there was one full-time USA based financial analyst assigned to support this business, supplemented by 4-5 relatively inexperienced remote analysts located in India.

Having worked directly with each of the remote analysts, I quickly realized they were financially book smart, but clearly lacked business knowledge and experience. In which case, their usefulness was limited through no fault of their own. Having been a financial analyst myself for several years, I can tell you that without an understanding of the business you are supporting, your usefulness will be limited at best. In retrospect, the India based resources should have been better trained regarding the intricacies of the business they were supporting.

Ultimately, we did resolve this issue, but not without classic overreaction that typically occurs in business when problems like this arise. Meaning, we added a bunch of Finance resources to support the BU. Although the business grew from $50M to $250M annual revenue within a few short years, I can safely say, we added far too many permanent Finance resources. Clearly some additional resources were needed, but we definitely went overboard. Furthermore, we moved the offshore support from India to Mexico. However, this time we did a much better job of providing the Mexico based financial analysts the necessary business and financial training. Without question, much of what we did was justified, and ultimately proved successful. However, it was definitely overkill. Meaning, we would likely have done equally well by only adding about half of those resources. Bottom line, whenever you end up with a situation in which checkers are checking the checkers and people are bumping into each other (figuratively speaking), you clearly have an over-abundant resource issue that must be addressed and rectified.

Once the additional resources were in place, any attempt to subsequently eliminate any of them would surely have been met with considerable resistance from the Deal P&L managers. As a matter of fact, the opposite was true with deal managers wanting even more financial support, mistakenly assuming that more is better. In economics this phenomenon is referred to as *the point of diminishing returns.* In other words, the point incremental cost going in is greater than the incremental value coming out, which in my opinion occurred at roughly the halfway point of this resource adding frenzy.

Incidentally, that was not the end of the Finance resource adding frenzy. The deal financial analysts were separate and distinct from the BU financial analysts, which the latter consisted of another dozen or so Finance resources. Some of those resources were on Country Finance Teams, while most others were on Region and Worldwide Finance Teams. Here again, as much as some additional resources were justified to support the growing business, management definitely went overboard. Incidentally, I must admit, essentially all of the added resources were high quality and hardworking people. Meaning, the individuals were not the problem. Instead, the problem was, once again, management overreacting to a resource need. The point of this story, business always comes down to the value proposition. Whenever you reach the point in which incremental cost exceeds incremental value, you are no longer helping the business. In fact, you are adversely affecting the bottom line.

Chapter 7

Internal vs. External Resources

Service Providers often utilize external resources to either augment their internal capabilities or in lieu of internal resources. The focus of this chapter is on when it makes more sense to use external versus internal resources. In this context, external resources refer to anyone other than employees. Therefore, consultants, temporary workers, as well as work that is outsourced to any number of specialty companies are all considered use of external resources. There are several cost factors that are often overlooked when managers consider using external resources. From what I have observed, the three most significant factors include: training, attrition, and management oversight cost. In order to create a true *apples-to-apples* comparison of external versus internal resource cost, the cost of these three factors must be added to the amount paid external resource vendors. Likewise, fringe plus all other employee-related overhead cost must be added to internal resource gross salary to reflect the fully burdened employee cost, which typically runs roughly 150% of gross salary.

Now let's discuss in more detail the three above mentioned commonly overlooked external versus internal cost factors, starting with management oversight. It's important to acknowledge the fact, there is a certain amount of management oversight required by the client (in this case the MSP) when utilizing external resources. Depending on the business arrangement between the client and vendor, there are various management oversight methods that can be utilized. One common method is on-going review of performance reports. In this case, if something looks odd or questionable in those reports, the client will meet with the vendor to discuss and resolve the odd/questionable issue(s). Other more formal client/vendor review methods are commonly referred to as Monthly Business Reviews (MBRs) or Quarterly Business Reviews (QBRs). In those cases, if there were few issues or problems that occurred during the period being reviewed, the time invested by the client will be limited. On the other hand, if there were significant issues or problems, the time invested by the client will be greater, resulting in higher management oversight cost. The fact of the matter, most outsourced work does not run perfectly smooth, making management oversight a critical component of all client/vendor business arrangements.

Next, let's talk about training cost that is associated with utilizing external resources. Responsibility for training external resources can vary along a full spectrum, from essentially being 100% client to 100% vendor responsibility. Nevertheless, the client will almost always have some level of involvement and, in some cases, incur substantial training cost. The most costly scenario for the client is when they are responsible for both creating and delivering all external resource training. A less costly scenario for them is when *train the trainer* approach is utilized. In which case, the client is only responsible for the initial training, while the vendor is responsible for all subsequent training. The least costly scenario for the client is when they are only responsible for creating the training material, and the vendor assumes full responsibility for delivering the training. Regardless of what approach is used, external training cost is clearly something that must be considered when contemplating use of external resources.

Finally, let's talk about attrition cost related to the use of external resources. Attrition rates can be especially significant in parts of the world where sought after low-cost resources are available such as India, China, Eastern Europe, and Central and South America. The reason being, many of those sought-after resources will typically move from one company to another for even the slightest wage increase, which is totally understandable considering the typical standard of living in many of those nations. Therefore, as resource movement increases, so too does attrition cost, primarily due to extraordinary training and ramp-up cost. Think about the cost difference of having, let's say, 5% versus roughly 30% annual attrition. It's important to be mindful, every time a new resource is brought into an organization, no matter how knowledgeable he may be, there will always be some training and ramp-up cost involved. So, if you are having to train 1 in 20 (5%) versus 1 in 3 (33%) external resources annually, training cost will be considerably different in those two extremes.

Admittedly, the use of external offshore resources is not nearly as common for MPS deals as it is for IT Infrastructure Managed Services deals, simply because the nature of the work is quite different. Nonetheless, it's not uncommon for Managed Print Services providers to leverage some level of low-cost offshore vendor resources for classic admin functions such as customer and billing admin, and other back-office processes.

When External Resources Make More Economic Sense

Regarding the fundamental question, when is it better to use external versus internal resources? The answer is, it depends on the company's tolerance for risk and willingness to deal with the usual challenges associated with pursuing a more cost competitive strategy. Let's start with risk, which is always a balancing act between rewards and consequences. Rewards are usually measured in terms of dollars, and consequences in terms of impact on customer satisfaction. It goes without saying, if you could take a risk lowering labor cost and not suffer corresponding customer satisfaction consequences, who wouldn't take that risk? Unfortunately, the reality of risk-taking is never knowing the outcome beforehand.

So, if you're planning to set up new externally supported activities or migrate existing internal activities to external resources, the best advice I can give is to be analytical and methodical with your approach. Start slow and constantly evaluate and tweak as necessary, while working toward completing the changeover. Going blindly and quickly can prove to be a costly mistake.

There are a number of reasons that can motivate companies to utilize external resources. One of the most popular reasons is desire to maximize profitability. Another popular reason is having to follow your competition to remain in the game (so to speak). The latter is not necessarily what one might consider a desirable reason, but intense competition can sometimes leave you with limited choices.

With regard to MPS businesses, I'd have to say the most common use of external resources is for field related work, which boils down to three specific activities. First, discovery of the client's existing environment, which can oftentimes be more economically done by a vendor that has locally available low-cost non-technical resources. Second, on-site hardware service and support, which might be done by authorized national or regional service providers. This is especially common when the MSP cannot leverage an internal Service & Support organization. The third activity vendors are commonly utilized is providing low-cost non-technical resources that take care of toner replacement, paper jambs, and other minor issues that may arise throughout the life of the MPS contract. These individuals are typically utilized in large client offices and campus sites. Whereas, in small offices and remote sites, the client's own resources typically handle these matters.

In addition to the above mentioned on-site support activities, MPS businesses may also use external resources for the following two reasons. One, offload mundane work from highly skilled, high-cost resources. And two, move back-office work to a more cost effective externally supported model. Let's talk about offloading mundane work first. With virtually no exceptions, all professional employees have to deal with a certain amount of mundane work, some more than others.

Let's consider the day-to-day activities of an ADM whose principal responsibility is overseeing and supporting a contracted client's environment. These relatively high paid individuals can easily consume a significant portion of their workday on mundane activities, in particular administrative paperwork. With enough complaints from ADMs about the extraordinary amount of precious time mundane work is consuming, executive managers will sometimes come to their rescue. When that happens, the first step usually taken is to create a list of ADM day-to-day activities along with the average amount of time each of those activities typically consumes. The next step is to separate *must keep* from *mundane* activities that can potentially be offloaded. Following those two steps, there is usually a lively management team discussion regarding the merits and risks of offloading each of the mundane activities, with particular emphases on potential impact to customer satisfaction. Once there is final agreement, a project plan is created listing all the activities that are to be offloaded in priority order. Normally, it's the so-called *low hanging fruit,* or activities expected to produce the biggest bang for the buck, that make it to the top of the list and are offloaded accordingly.

And finally, let's talk about offloading back-office work, which typically represents the least amount of risk for the MPS business. Examples of back-office work in those businesses include: contract administration, billing, asset management, and more. Furthermore, moving those relatively straightforward administrative functions generally involve less training cost, which is particularly important if the functions are being moved to developing countries where attrition is expected to be extraordinarily high.

Offloading back-office work is usually handled one of two ways. The first, enter into a contractual agreement with a low-cost service provider who will do the work from an offshore or near-shore location. The second, keep the work internally, but move it to a newly created Center of Excellence in an offshore or near-shore location. The latter option may require some capital investment, including brick and mortar cost, or possibly a long-term building lease arrangement. However, given the fact investments can be capitalized and depreciated over a long period of time, the internal Center of Excellence may well turn out to be the better option. Ultimately, what matters most is, which option offers the best and most cost effective solution. Bottom line, whether the work is done by a vendor or internal Center of Excellence, offloading back-office work to an offshore or near-shore location has generally proven to be an effective cost reduction strategy.

Let's face it, virtually anything that's done internally by employees can also be done externally by consultants or contractors. Therefore, a decision to offload work to external resources usually comes down to where the work can be done better, faster, cheaper, while maintained desired quality, security, and customer satisfaction levels. Incidentally, decisions to offload work can be complicated and oftentimes emotionally charged. Some of the contributing factors might include such things as: managers attempting to protect their employees, local or national politics, pressure from special interest groups, etc. Also, it's important to point out that emotion and resistance run hottest when a company is considering sending the work outside national borders. Whereas, there is generally more tolerance and less resistance when the work is being offloaded to low-cost areas within national borders. Whether that is due to patriotism, nationalism, or else, decision makers should anticipate encountering some resistance whenever contemplating moving work offshore.

From what I have observed, the attitude and willingness to utilize external resources has changed dramatically over the past several years, principally due to competitive cost pressures. More and more companies are looking externally for low-cost resource solutions just to remain competitive. Of course, there are other companies that address competitive challenges with advanced technology and automation. However, in service businesses, there is usually a limit how far advanced technology and automation will take you. The fact of the matter, service businesses are essentially people cost businesses. In which case, if those companies want to materially impact cost, they have to deal with difficult people related decisions, which oftentimes results in leveraging low-cost external resources.

Apples to Apples Internal vs. External Cost Comparison

Whenever you are doing an internal versus external resource cost comparison, your internal cost must take into account all employee-related expenses, including fringe and all other employee overhead. As previously mentioned, fully burdened employee cost typically runs approximately 150% of gross salary. Similarly, external resource cost must consider factors beyond just what you pay your resource vendor. Depending on where the external resources are actually located, you may incur physical accommodation costs for such things as: office space, phone, network, etc. You will also incur management oversight cost, which we discussed the details earlier. The point being, for a realistic *apples to apples* cost comparison, all applicable internal and external resource related cost must be taken into account.

Depending on the type of agreement you have with the resource vendor, you will likely be paying based on one of the following methods: actual hours worked, a dedicated individual(s), or contracted deliverables. These three methods by no means represent a complete list of payment options. There are numerous other arrangements that can be made, limited only by what is agreeable to both client and vendor. For discussion purposes, we are going to limit our focus to the three above mentioned methods, including the pros and cons of each method.

Paying for hours worked is both a straightforward and convenient payment method. However, the downside of this method, there is usually no guarantee client desired quality and/or quantity levels will be met. Meaning, the vendor could deliver undesirable quality and/or insufficient quantity of service without consequences. Generally speaking, hourly payment arrangements are especially common for unskilled and low-level professional workers.

Paying for a dedicated individual(s) is another straightforward payment method. However, this too does not guarantee desired quality and/or quantity performance levels will be met. Allow me to explain myself. Naturally, when a dedicated individual is hired for a given task or project, there is a presumption predefined deliverables will be met. The fact of the matter, whether or not those deliverables are actually met is dependent on the quality and the knowledge level of the external resource brought in to do the work. The only thing that is certain with this type of arrangement, the client is locked into paying for the external resource, regardless of actual accomplishments. Therefore, a notable drawback with this payment method, the client could end up making a significant investment with no guarantee deliverables will actually be met. That is the reason this payment method realistically only makes sense for time-based deliverables. For example, an interim substitute for an internal resource that may be taking a medical or maternity leave.

The last payment method we will discuss is paying for contracted projects, which typically include milestones and completion parameters. What matters most in this type of arrangement is getting the job done right and on time. In other words, achieving deliverables that are bound by time constraints and predefined service level parameters (commonly referred to as SLAs). The most notable benefit of this payment method, it essentially guarantees the project will be done as expected and on time. Otherwise, the resource vendor will suffer the related financial consequences, meaning being paid less or not paid at all for the project. And, worse yet, potentially experience non-performance penalties, if they are included in the contract.

Now I'd like to briefly turn our attention to the pros and cons of utilizing an existing internal resource to handle a specific project or assignment, assuming of course that individual possesses the required knowledge and skills. From a pros standpoint, there is generally no *real* incremental cost involved when a company utilizes an existing resource. The principal reason, that individual is already included in the company payroll. Another pro, there are definitely less security and quality control concern when an internal resource is utilized. From a cons standpoint, all a manager can realistically do is specify the required project goals. Whether or not those goals are actually achieved depends on the employee's knowledge, skills, motivation and drive.

Another con is related to a newly hired internal resource that is brought on board to handle a specific project. At some point, that project will be completed. Then what happens to that resource? Sure, there may be some other projects that individual can work on. But, will they be worthwhile from a value perspective, or will they simply keep the individual busy? In some situations, company management may decide that individual is no longer needed. When that happens, they will likely be faced with a related financial challenge, specifically, separation (or severance) cost. Bottom line, there are potential risks associated with all hiring decisions, whether they are for internal or external resources. That is why all resource decisions must be handled with considerable thought, care, and foresight. Otherwise, those decisions may prove regrettable from both a human impact and business profit standpoint.

Low-cost Offshore Resources Not Always Best Choice

Low-cost offshore resources are enticing for companies who are participating in a competitive market or simply attempting to improve profitability. On the other hand, there are inherent risks associated with offshoring, which decision makers must be mindful and prepared to confront. It's important to be aware that successful offshore solutions require a considerable amount of effort to go into the planning, design, and rollout phases. And, in order to maximize positive outcome, there must be a willingness to adjust or tweak the offshore solution after it's been rolled out.

Among the biggest challenges companies face implementing a successful offshore solution are quality control and attracting and retaining qualified resources. Quality control is usually influenced by the quality of the training, and of course, the knowledge and skill level of the offshore resources who are actually doing the work. We already discussed at length the importance of training, which the same basic principles apply to training offshore resources. Therefore, let's move on to the challenge of attracting and retaining qualified resources.

Typically, when you go into a low-cost developing country that has well-educated professional resources, you are not the only company in town looking for those resources. You are sure to find other companies competing for those same precious resources. In which case, the companies that are willing to pay the highest wages usually attract the lion's share of the resources. The primary reason, most people in developing countries are struggling to improve their basic living standards. Therefore, earned wages are of utmost importance. Furthermore, most individuals will not think twice about moving from one company to another, even for a modest wage increase. The resulting extraordinary attrition will exacerbate incremental hiring, training, and development cost that will have to be incurred on replacement resources. The more complex the position, the bigger the challenge and higher the replacement cost. So, if your company is not willing or able to deal with these challenges, which some are admittedly frustrating, offshoring will likely not be a viable solution.

There is one final point I'd like to make regarding this matter. Just as with any other support solution, the knowledge and skill level of the offshore resources brought on board matters. In which case, finding desired caliber resources in a given local market can be challenging. The primary reason, the availability of those resources is heavily influenced by local economies and especially the presence of higher education institutions that fuel supply. Bangalore, India is a perfect example of a location with abundant knowledgeable and highly skilled resources. The principal reason, they have several outstanding technical universities fueling availability. The same cannot be said for many other developing countries that offer low-cost resources. My point being, if you're planning to take advantage of an offshore support solution, be mindful of local knowledge and skill limitations that may exist. Furthermore, when supply is limited, you should expect more competition for those resources. Meaning, you should be prepared to pay competitively higher wages.

At this point, I'd like to share an example of an offshore support quality challenge, which I made reference to earlier. A few years back, I joined a BU that was leveraging offshore financial resources to support USA based contracted services deals. Like most businesses who are constantly looking for ways to lower cost and improve profitability, this organization decided to switch from local to offshore financial analysts. Frankly, the solution was doomed to failure from the very beginning for two reasons.

First, training the offshore resources was the responsibility of an already overburdened USA based financial analyst. Considering all of the other important day-to-day responsibilities this individual had, his plate was already full (so to speak). Therefore, remotely training people from half way around the globe was simply not a priority. Second, just like most things that are done with lack of sufficient time and marginal interest, the resulting training turned out to be grossly inadequate. In retrospect, once I learned about this individual's time struggle, I'd say the outcome was predictable. The blame for failure did not rest with that individual or the offshore resources. Management was clearly at fault for not committing sufficient resources to a decision they made.

Vendors Must Be Accountable for End-client Deliverables

From a best practices standpoint, most external resource agreements should include clearly outlined deliverables and performance goals. When external resources are hired by a middleman like an MSP, the deliverables and performance goals the MSP is accountable to the end-client should also be reflected in the agreement between the external resource vendor and the

MSP. That way, both parties share responsibility for achieving end-client deliverables, as well as risk of potentially incurring non-performance penalties.

I have seen cases in which contracts with third party resource vendors are loosely defined and less stringent than the deliverables the MSP was accountable to the end-client. Worse yet, I've seen other cases in which there was no mention of end-client deliverables in the agreement between the resource vendor and the MSP. Under either of the given circumstances, if the resource vendor is reliable and provides high quality resources, there is no harm done. On the other hand, if the resource vendor is not reliable and end-client deliverables are not met, the situation can become costly for the MSP. In extreme cases, the MSP may also run the risk of losing the end-client. Bottom line, it behooves all parties involved to use very clear and unambiguous contract language outlining responsibilities and accountabilities. Furthermore, it's always best when everyone involved in end-client deliverables are focused on achieving the same results and have some skin in the game.

Part III

Managing the Financials

Chapter 8

Plan of Record (POR) Deal P&Ls

At this point, we're going to start a very detailed discussion regarding MPS profitability management, with particular emphasis on Deal P&L management. Deal P&Ls are essential for a number of reasons, most of all to identify contracts that are contributing to profit versus those that are eating profit. In this chapter we're going to talk about the Plan of Record (POR) P&L, which represents the contracted deal final solution P&L. In particular, we're going to discuss the various shortcomings and challenges associated with POR P&Ls. In the next chapter we will have a lengthy discussion regarding Actual Deal P&L management, including the criticality of financial integrity and the necessity P&L managers possess a good understanding of transaction source data. Most importantly, we will do a deep dive into how Deal P&L managers can leverage available levers and knobs to improve deal profitability. And finally, we will discuss what those managers can do to increase contracted deal size and scope. In the last chapter of Part III, we're going to talk about Forecast Deal P&Ls, including best practice forecasting processes and tools.

Incidentally, it's important to point out, although the total MPS business may be profitable, that does not mean each of the contracted deals in the portfolio is profitable. As a matter of fact, the opposite is generally true. Therefore, having the ability to produce and analyze deal level P&Ls allows managers to make better informed decisions, particularly regarding challenging deals.

In business, profitability measurement and management are important from multiple points of view. Regardless of whether your contracted services business is big or small, a separate BU inside a large product company, or a standalone services company, it's critical to know whether or not each deal in your portfolio is profitable. Therefore, having the necessary tools, systems, and processes in place to create accurate and reliable deal level P&Ls is a foundational requirement. In addition to the total business and deal level P&Ls, most contracted service businesses produce summary P&Ls for the various regions and countries they operate. Given the latter P&Ls are strictly summary views, I have no intention of discussing them in greater detail.

One of the principal documents created during MPS deal negotiations and approval process is the POR P&L. Generally, there are several revisions of the POR P&L created throughout the deal solution process. Once the deal is approved, the final POR P&L is considered one of the most important reference documents, which Actual and Forecast P&Ls are constantly compared throughout the entire life of the deal. As you might imagine, there are several things considered before a deal is finally approved. For example, deal size and scope, the client's strategic importance, desire to penetrate a particular business sector, etc. Nevertheless, how good or bad the POR P&L looks will predominately determine whether or not the deal is approved. Generally speaking, MSPs establish predetermined minimum gross margin threshold guidelines, which must be met or exceeded in order for a deal to be approved. Approval of deals that have planned gross margin below those thresholds require progressively higher level executive management sign-off. For example, the guidelines may state that country managers can approve deals that are at or above the predefined gross margin threshold. Deals that are up to 5% below that threshold must be approved by WW region managers (in other words, the Americas, EMEA, or Asia Pacific region managers), and deals with planned gross margin bellow that must be approved by Global Management.

POR Shortcomings

From my experience, the bigger the deal, most often the lower is the planned gross margin. Why? Because those are precisely the deals Managed Services Providers compete fiercely to win. There are all sorts of fancy notions and reams of accompanying marketing material produced that claim differentiating qualities amongst the MSPs. Although some of those claims are true, for the most part they represent more marketing than substance. It's naïve to think otherwise, especially when MPS solutions essentially utilize commodity products and more or less standard software. The harsh reality, all things considered, winning is mostly about price. The more competitive the MSP price, the more likely that vendor will win the deal.

In many of those highly competitive situations, the winner often ends up with nothing more than a complicated big revenue deal that produces low profit margin. In most cases, those deals have to be intently managed for the next several years just to keep it on the positive side of break-even. So, tell me, who is the real winner in these very competitive big deals? The answer is, the savvy client who is able to effectively play MSPs against one another and ultimately obtain the best possible deal and price. I am not suggesting MSPs not pursue competitive mega deals. However, I am stating, the mistaken notion that low margin mega deal revenue is going to contribute to portfolio profitability is, for the most part, a costly illusion.

Unprofitable or low margin revenue has never, and will never, help a company achieve long-term financial success. I have been responsible for Managed Services deal portfolios that included the full spectrum of deal sizes: small, medium, large, and mega deals. Without exception, the deals that required the most management attention and presented the biggest strain on portfolio gross margin were the mega deals. Conversely, the deals that required the least amount of attention, and made the most contribution to portfolio gross margin were the small and medium deals with standard deliverables. In fact, the small and medium deals typically ended up subsidizing the mega deals from a profitability perspective.

So, why is it that MSPs want to win highly competitive mega deals? In many cases, to grow the P&L top line. In other cases, to establish presents or dominance in a particular business sector, for example banking. Whatever the reasons, the MSP must be careful not to load up their portfolio with too many of these big revenue low margin deals. The reason being, their weight will surely sink the ship (so to speak). Frankly, other than adding a logo to a portfolio, I never truly understood what *real* contribution these mega deals make to the business, other than creating perpetual heartburn for the people responsible for managing the deals and putting pressure on portfolio gross margin.

POR challenges

In addition to representing the approved financial plan for contracted services deals, POR P&Ls are utilized throughout the life of the deal to compare against Actual and Forecast P&Ls. One of the principal responsibilities of Deal P&L owners is ensuring actual gross margin meets or exceeds POR. Otherwise, they will be required to provide sound reasoning why their deal is not achieving plan. And, more importantly, demonstrate to management how they plan to get the deal back on track with quantifiable profit improvement initiatives. As you might imagine, the further negative actual deals are from planned gross margin, the more often Deal P&L owners have to face management to explain progress being made toward achieving committed corrective actions (the improvement initiatives).

Red/yellow/green dashboards are commonly used to demonstrate the severity of deal gross margin problems. In which case, red accounts are reviewed monthly or quarterly, yellow accounts are reviewed semi-annually, and green accounts are reviewed annually. As you can see, this can easily turn into an endless vicious cycle for poorly performing deals. Lucky are the green account managers who are left alone to concentrate on managing clients and further improving their deal financial performance. Whereas, yellow and, in particular, red account managers waste precious cycles preparing and delivering countless management updates, and are constantly grilled to do more and faster.

The reality of the situation, more often than not and through no fault of his own, the Deal P&L owner ends up being the victim in highly competitive and poorly conceived deal solutions. As mentioned earlier, competition to win big deals is usually intense. The bigger the deal, the more intense the competition and longer the sale and solution cycle. Allow me to share a real-life scenario, which I have repeatedly witnessed.

The Solution team, which is on point for winning these big deals, will often engineer progressively more challenging ways to remain in the competitive bidding process, even if the solution assumptions are far-fetched and unrealistic. After all, it's all about winning, isn't it? Ultimately, the deal is won and the Solution team receives kudos for doing a great job, coupled with of course their incentive compensation. So, everyone is happy, right? Surely not the Deal P&L owner who is faced with the long-term challenge of turning those far-fetched assumptions into deliverable realities. Not exactly an enviable position to be in, which is precisely the reason the first and sometimes even second deal delivery manager is replaced. The lesson here, put a person in a position to achieve the impossible, and the inevitable will happen.

Let me give you a couple examples of impossible solution assumptions. The first, a solution calls for four-hour on-site response and eight-hour resolution time for the entire client environment, including several isolated locations throughout the nation. The fact of the matter, the in-house delivery organization is simply not set up to provide that level of service. In order to do so, delivery management can do one of two things. Hire additional in-house resources or engage with regional or national third-party service providers to deliver on-site support in those isolated client locations. Taking either of those two steps will result in unplanned spending, which will obviously put pressure on the deal gross margin.

The second impossible solution assumption is related to revenue instead of cost. In a Managed Print Services solution, one of the key assumptions is number of printed pages. Meaning, in order for the deal to be profitable, the client has to print enough pages to absorb the MSP's fixed cost. In this case, the Solution team makes an exaggerated assumption regarding the projected number of printed pages, knowing full well the customer will never even get close to actually printing that number of pages.

So, you might be wondering, how does the Solution team get away with making impossible or unrealistic assumptions without being called on the carpet (so to speak)? In most cases, pre-contract due diligence is limited to some, but not all existing customer sites. Therefore, it's entirely possible for the Solution team to extrapolate from favorable due diligence sites, resulting in inflated deal projected volumes. Sure, that may be a little underhanded, but winning is what matters most. Scary, isn't it? Although no one will openly admit to doing so, I can assure you things like I just described occur in desperately sought-after wins. How do I know that? The proof is blatantly obvious after the deal is rolled out and actual printed page reports are generated. If actual printed pages are significantly lower than the solution assumption, something must be fundamentally wrong. Wouldn't you agree? It's only after the fact, when the Solution team is challenged regarding how they arrived at the projected printed pages that management realized some underhanded behavior must have occurred during the deal solution process.

I realize that I may be coming across a little harsh here. But I assure you, there is good reason for doing so. I have seen the very thing I just described occur numerous times. And, I have always been on the receiving end of the problem, meaning the delivery team. The fact of the matter, these planned Deal P&Ls are pretty much the bible when it comes to performance expectations. Unfortunately, many of them are riddled with unrealistic solution assumptions, making achieving the deal plan essentially impossible. And, good luck to the people who are accountable for making the impossible happen, which in this case would be the deal delivery and/or client manager. Bottom line, there are only two winners in these illusionary big deal solutions. First, the savvy client who plays competitors against one another to get the best possible deal and price. Second, the deal Solution team members who receive incentive compensation for winning deals, even when they are bad deals.

With regard to the latter, this is an age-old problem in Managed Services businesses, which can only be addressed through more restrictive incentive compensation plans. The worst thing a company can do is give the Solution team members 100% of their incentive compensation when the deal is signed. A better approach would be to split the incentive. Let's say 50% when the deal is signed, and the other 50% one year later when actual gross margins can be compared to plan. An even better approach might be using annual milestones for the first three years of the deal life. In which case, you might award 25% at deal signing and 25% at the completion of each of the first three years of the contract life. That way, Solution team members would receive incentive compensation that is more in line with actual versus planned deal gross margin performance for those three years. The idea being, the better or worse gross margin the deal generates, the higher or lower incentive compensation the Solution team members would be eligible.

Chapter 9

Managing Actual Deal P&Ls

Actual Deal P&Ls provide both a historical view of financial performance, as well as a means of measuring actual profitability against the approved deal plan (POR). However, without drilling down into the related details, you cannot simply look at a Deal P&L and determine which business drivers are having a positive versus a negative impact on profitability, something we're going to talk more about shortly. Furthermore, it's important to point out, although a deal portfolio may be producing a healthy overall margin that does not mean each individual deal in the portfolio is doing the same. As previously mentioned, the opposite is generally true. You are almost guaranteed to find some losers in most portfolios, which means you have to drill down into the details to determine why some deals are profitable and others are not.

Most of us have heard the proverbial *trees in the forest* saying. Well, I have my own twist on that famous saying as it applies to Deal P&Ls. Let's assume you're flying a small single engine plane over a forest at 2,000 feet. The forest may look pretty good from that height. That is to say, your Portfolio P&L (the forest) looks good in its entirety. So, you may be thinking to yourself, *I'm a solid P&L manager, able to produce, let's say, 25% gross margin, while the other portfolio managers are producing 20% or less.* You may also be thinking, *management should appreciate and reward me for the excellent job I am doing managing my portfolio profitability,* and they should.

But, here is the thing about the trees in the forest. This good-looking forest has some broken trees and twisted branches, which are not visible from 2,000 feet. That is to say, there are individual deals in your portfolio that are not performing well, with some actually generating negative gross margin. Clearly, those troubled deals require individual attention to attempt to bring them back to profitability. Unfortunately, that will simply not be possible with some deals. In which case, the best course of action is to start taking a much closer look at those poorly performing deals. In situations there are no viable improvement options, your best course of action may be breaking off the contracts with those clients. Of course, you would have to consider cancellation and/or other potential penalties that might apply. Also, if it's a client your company is doing business on multiple fronts, you need to take a more holistic view and consider how your actions might impact the overall client relationship. Ultimately, you would only take the suggested action if it's financially prudent, and you are confident it will not have broader negative ramifications.

Another less disruptive way of dealing with financially troubled deals is to *not* renew them. The fact of the matter, without Actual Deal P&Ls, you have no way of knowing which deals are good and which deals are bad from a financial perspective. Worse yet, there is a good chance you may renew unprofitable deals simply because you have no way of knowing otherwise. When that happens, you have locked yourself in for an additional five years of losses (assuming it's a five-year renewal deal). Think about what a hero you would be if you had the ability to leverage deal specific P&Ls to further improve your portfolio profitability. Depending on the number of bad deals in your portfolio, there may be ways to gradually start driving up profitability from 25% to, let's say, eventually 30%. At that point, management would definitely be obligated to do something more than simply say "thank you" along with an accompanying pat on the back. A promotion with more money, or at minimum a sizable incentive compensation check for outstanding performance would definitely be in order.

When we think about Actual Deal P&Ls, it's important to be mindful of three important points. First, reliable P&Ls start and end with financial integrity. Without integrity, P&Ls are misleading and potentially dangerous because many business decisions are influenced by the company's P&L results. Second, you can't fix something you don't understand, meaning you cannot effectively manage and control deal profitability if you don't have a good handle on source data. Third, it's essential that you also have a good handle on business drivers. That is to say, ability to leverage and control available levers and knobs that will help improve deal profitability. Beyond that, there is only one other major thing the account manager should be concerned. Specifically, increasing deal size and scope while maintaining or improving customer satisfactions. Next, we're going to discuss the four above mentioned points in more detail.

Reliable Deal P&Ls Start and End with Financial Integrity

The single most important quality of reliable financial performance reporting is integrity. We have all heard the old adage, *garbage in garbage out*. Truer words could not be said regarding P&L integrity. Without integrity, P&Ls are not only misleading, they are potentially downright dangerous. The reason being, many business decisions are influenced by P&L results. Data integrity is not something that accidentally happens. It must be engrained into the company culture. For example, as mundane as account coding may be, it is a common source of data integrity issues. Therefore, businesses must make sure employees are properly trained on account coding dos and don'ts. There are of course several other factors that affect data integrity. That said, next we're going to talk about common factors that affect Deal P&L accuracy and reliability. We're going to start with factors that affect revenue, followed by factors that affect cost.

Customer billing is unquestionably the most significant factor that affects revenue. In which case, the accuracy of Deal P&L reporting is only as good as the customer name and number coding on billing transactions. As obvious is that may appear to be, it's a problem in most large companies. Why, you might be wondering? Throughout my professional career, I have worked in four major international corporations. I have never seen what I would characterize as a streamlined and efficient customer master data management process. In fact, I have seen the complete opposite. For the same customer, there have literally been as many as a half dozen or more name variations set up in the customer master database, with each having a different customer number assignment. Simply put, this unfortunate phenomenon occurs because of lacking or loosely defined customer master data administrative processes.

The following scenario is a typical example of how this particular problem is exacerbated. Instead of searching the customer master database for an existing customer name, careless administrators simply go ahead and set up a new customer name as reflected in the paperwork they have in front of them. Done enough times, you can see how this undisciplined behavior can easily lead to an out-of-control customer master database. Here is an example of what I am referring. A company like General Electric might have the following name variations in the customer master database: General Electric Company, GE Co., General Electric, GE, etc. You get the idea. The reason I'm telling you this, if business transactions are not coded with the correct customer name and number, the Deal P&L for that client will be misstated. Furthermore, costly and cumbersome manual intervention will be required to correct the reporting problem (as in manual journal entries). Obviously, this type of problem can be avoided if there is more care and attention applied to the upfront administrative process.

Cost related financial integrity factors are more numerous than revenue factors, particularly as it applies to Deal P&L integrity. In which case, the single most important thing that can be done is set up a dedicated cost center for each contracted deal in the General Ledger. That way, all deal related cost (except allocated overhead) will be captured in the designated cost center, and reflected in the corresponding Deal P&L. Without dedicated cost centers, the cost reflected on Deal P&Ls will likely be based on various allocation methodologies, which never result in the same level of accuracy and reliability.

Generally speaking, there are two ways of getting cost assigned to Deal P&Ls. You can do it on an actual transaction basis or allocation basis. The more cost that is allocated, the less accurate and reliable you should expect the Deal P&Ls to be. Let me give you an example. Let's assume you have an MPS portfolio with 100 deals. Let's further assume on-site service for those deals is provided by an internal company Service & Support organization. At the end of each month, your deal portfolio is charged with a single cost entry for all the service transactions related to deals in your portfolio. In which case, it's up to you to decide how to allocate portions of that cost to each of the Deal P&Ls in your portfolio. One common allocation methodology is to base it on the percentage of total revenue each deal generated. Another common methodology is to base it on the percentage of total cost each deal incurred. Of course, there are other ways to allocate cost, but the two given methods are among the most common. Using either of these so-called *peanut butter spread* methods are imperfect at best. And, they will almost certainly result in inaccurate Deal P&Ls, which will ultimately result in poorly informed business decisions.

Instead of allocating on-site support cost, with a little more data capture and reporting effort, your Deal P&Ls can be much more accurate and reliable. Virtually all organizations that provide on-site support utilize a service application system.

Those systems are used to dispatch service technicians, as well as capture incident data and accompanying cost, such as: end-client customer name, service technician name, repair time and cost, travel time and cost, parts used and cost, etc. Leveraging deal specific incident data to book actual on-site service cost to each Deal P&L is obviously more accurate and reliable than allocating cost. Ideally, you would want to automate this process by linking the service application system to the General Ledger, and have actual cost posted directly to deal cost centers. If automation is not possible, the next best thing is to generate a detailed incident report from the service application system, sorted by customer/deal name. Then use that report to book charges to each deal cost center via manual journal entries. Either way (automated or manual), I guarantee Deal P&Ls will be much more accurate and reliable than any allocation methodology that might otherwise be used.

There are numerous other examples of financial data integrity issues and challenges I could share with you, which I will limit to just one more in a moment. As mentioned earlier, financial integrity is not something that accidentally happens. It requires deliberate actions supported by sound business processes and procedures. And yes, in some cases that may mean a little extra work or effort from the individuals involved. In other cases, it may mean investing in some additional automation. In the final analysis, management needs to decide how critical versus costly is ensuring financial data integrity. The more business decisions are based on financial results, the more important is financial data integrity. Simply put, if you can effectively manage your business as an aggregate unit, the types of financial data integrity we are discussing is not terribly important. On the other hand, if it's important that you manage contracted deal financial performance, these types of data integrity issues are critically important.

Now let's get to that last example I promised. This one has to do with a cost distribution problem resulting from miscoded Purchase Orders (POs). A problem I have seen repeatedly occur on POs that were issued to third party service and resource vendors. In this case, account coding is important for several reasons, most of all, getting cost assigned to the right deal cost center. Oftentimes, the PO originator does not reside in the cost center the charges are intended. Let's say the originator is a transition manager that is assigned to a shared resource cost center. And, the intended cost center is one that is assigned to a particular contracted deal.

Let's assume the transition manager generates a PO for temporary external resources to help with the deal transition effort. A common problem that occurs, the transition manager inadvertently codes the PO with his own cost center instead of the deal cost center. Hence, when the vendor payments are made against that PO, the charges end up in the shared resource cost center instead of the intended deal cost center. When that happens, the only way to fix the problem is with manual intervention, meaning reclassifying the cost via a manual journal entry. Worse yet, problems that are not discovered contribute to misstated Deal P&Ls. Here again, we are dealing with a classic case of lacking or loosely defined business processes. The best way to prevent this type of problem from occurring in the first place is with enhanced employee communication and training.

Understanding Transaction Source Data

You can't fix something you don't understand. That is to say, you cannot effectively manage and control deal profitability if you don't understand the related transactions source data. Let's first talk about the different sources of services financial data. Essentially, there are three sources, listed in the order of preference: 1) integrated reporting databases, 2) individual application system databases, and 3) spreadsheets and manual transactions such as journal entries. In an ideal situation, a company would have an integrated reporting database with robust capability, from which they could pull detailed financial transaction reports, as well as various other standard and ad hoc reports, including on demand Deal P&Ls. Incidentally, the reporting database would be periodically updated (whether that be daily, weekly, or monthly) with transaction data from a number of independent business application system feeds.

The next best way of getting to source data is directly from independent business application system databases. In other words, this would be a non-integrated solution that requires more work pulling and making sense of the fragmented reporting data. The least desirable way of getting to source data is from makeshift spreadsheets and individual manual transactions such as journal entries. Obviously, the second and third methods are not nearly as efficient as the first. The fact of the matter, not every business can afford to have an integrated reporting database solution. Particularly small and medium size services companies who are often struggling with mere existence. Nevertheless, the more automated and integrated the database solution, the more efficient and better quality will be the reported data.

Now let's talk about taking action to address challenges revealed from source data reports. Let's assume you are a delivery manager responsible for a large MPS deal that utilizes embedded leases for the hardware placed at your client's sites. As mentioned earlier, embedded leases mean you (the MSP) are the lessee, and the lessor is either an internal leasing organization or an external financing company. Either way, you are the one responsible for the hardware lease payments, while your client simply pays for the bundled services you provide. For example, in an MPS deal your client might pay per printed page, without regard to how much hardware is in their environment.

Let's assume you are an account manager for an MPS deal that includes 100 leased printers. Shortly after the initial installation, three pieces of equipment experience hard failure, requiring replacement. So, you contact the leasing company and they arrange to send you three replacement units. Given all the things you currently have on your plate, including successfully completing a major transition, you forget about the three failed units. On the other hand, the leasing company couldn't care less about your personal challenges. All they care about is that you now have 103 hardware units located at your client's sites, for which they will gladly continue billing you monthly leasing charges. The fact that you failed to call them to request an MRA to return the failed units does not concern them in the least.

Now, let's get back to the related reporting. As delivery manager responsible for your Deal P&L, you have access to detailed monthly lease billing reports showing the amount billed for each piece of hardware that is assigned to your deal. If you take time to review the report, you will quickly realize that you are being billed for 103 units, instead of just the 100 active units in your client's environment. If you want future billing to stop for those three units, you have to request an MRA to get the failed units back to the leasing company. On the other hand, if you ignore the lease billing report because you're too busy with other matters, you will continue paying for those three non-functioning units as long as they continue to go unnoticed. Or, at least until you finally take the time to review and act on the lease billing report. The simple fact is, reviewing the lease billing report and taking appropriate and timely action to return the three failed units will definitely have a favorable impact on your Deal P&L.

Another example of taking action (or not) to address a challenge revealed in reported source data is related to a questionable shared labor charge from the Labor Tracking & Costing system. As delivery manager responsible for a Deal P&L, you have access to labor cross-charge reports, which contain the following details: shared resource names, hours worked, cross-charge amounts, and more. Let's assume you are either too busy with other matters, or simply not interested looking at detailed labor cross-charge reports. The fact of the matter, ignoring those reports may cost your Deal P&L dearly. How, you might wonder? I cannot tell you the number of times I've seen two predominant error types occur that are related to cross-charges for shared resources. Neither of these problems are caused intentionally by the person entering data into the Labor Tracking & Costing tool. Nevertheless, those cross-charges resulted in financial posting errors. Before getting into the error details, allow me to remind you about two fundamental facts. One, we are all human and humans make mistakes. Two, it's important to always be mindful that the quality of the output is only as good as the quality of input data.

Now let's talk about those two predominant error types. One is a cost center coding error, meaning labor is charged to the wrong deal cost center. Think about it. Your MPS business has a sizable shared services organization with hundreds of individuals charging time (cost) to the deals they are supporting. On any given week or month, a single shared resource could be alternating his time among several separate deals. In those situations, it's not hard to imagine how an honest mistake could be made coding a labor charge to the wrong deal cost center. In which case, if the cost center owner does not review the labor cross-charge report, an unintentional coding error could easily slip through the cracks and adversely impact his Deal P&L.

The second predominant error that occurs is the so-called *fat finger error.* In this case, let's assume an intended 10 hours input was accidentally entered as 100 hours. As the saying goes, what's an extra zero amongst friends? Let's do the math and see. Assuming a fully burdened labor rate for the individual charging time to the deal is $100/hour, that fat finger error cost the P&L owner an additional $9,000 (90 hours @ $100/hour). This is another example of what would have been time well spent by the delivery manager who was on the receiving end of the erroneous charge. Once again, this example proves that taking time to review source data reports can certainly be worthwhile. Listen, I've been there. I am very familiar with the everyday struggles a delivery manager faces. It's always a juggling act, deciding what to work on and what to ignore. In most cases, a delivery manager has more things to do than time available in the workday. However, somehow or another he must either find the time or assign someone the task of reviewing key operations management reports, which could prove consequential if they are ignored.

Managing Profit Improvement Levers and Knobs

Beyond ensuring financial integrity and having a good understanding of the source data, equally important improving contracted deal profitability is focusing on business drivers. Business drivers mean different things to different people, and in a broad sense can include any number of both internal and external factors. Our focus will be primarily on internal business drivers that impact MPS contracted deal revenue and cost. As Deal P&L owner, if you do nothing to influence those business drivers, like it or not, you will live with the resulting P&L. On the other hand, managing available levers and knobs will almost guarantee improved Deal P&L performance, something we will discuss in considerable detail shortly.

Just to get grounded, let's look at an example of a business driver. In most businesses, customer billing is naturally the principal revenue driver. However, it's important to understand that what you bill your customer may very well be different than the amount of revenue reflected in your P&L. The reason being, in some cases you may be billing in arrears (for past months), and in other cases you may be billing in advance (for future months). Arrears billing is reported as revenue the month the billing occurs, regardless of how many backdated months are involved. Incidentally, arrears (or back-billing) typically occurs as a result of administrative paperwork processing delays.

On the other hand, advanced billing for an upcoming quarter or year is not reported as earned revenue the month it's billed. Instead, the revenue is deferred. Meaning, it is incrementally recognized in future months, when the corresponding cost is incurred. My intention here is not to get into accounting weeds, which I know many people are uncomfortable. I'm simply pointing out the fact that you cannot look at a billing report and presume the amount billed will be reflected as current month revenue in the P&L. Now let's talk briefly about negative revenue, which typically means you are dealing with some kind of a customer credit. Just like back billing, customer credits are reported as negative revenue the month the credit is processed, regardless of how many backdated months may be involved.

At this point, I'd like to start a comprehensive discussion about the impact managing available levers and knobs can potentially have on improving deal profitability. The best way to accomplish that is by sharing pertinent real-life experiences, including the encountered challenges and resolution recommendations. Let's assume you are a delivery manager who has P&L responsibility for a large MPS deal that is currently only marginally profitable. In which case, you have been tasked with finding ways to improve your deal profitability to a more acceptable level. Let's further assume this is a standard MPS deal with hardware, supplies and service P&L components, and the hardware financing is handled via embedded leases. Remember, an embedded lease is a contract between the financing organization (the lessor) and the MSP (the lessee). In MPS deals, the end-client indirectly pays for leased hardware via one of several possible bundled billing options. Finally, let's assume this particular end-client has printers located in three large campus sites and numerous small remote sites. The best way to tackle this challenge is by systematically analyzing the revenue and cost drivers that impact each of the three P&L components, including hardware, supplies, and service. We'll start with hardware revenue drivers, followed by hardware cost drivers. We will then talk about supplies revenue and cost drivers, and finally service revenue and cost drivers.

Hardware revenue is driven by device placement, meaning the hardware must be installed and operational before revenue and cost can be reported on MPS (pro-forma) Deal P&Ls. This may sound a little unusual to many of you who are accustomed to seeing hardware revenue and cost recorded when product is shipped. Allow me to digress for a moment to explain the reason it's done this way for MPS (pro-forma) Deal P&L reporting purposes. In this case, I am referring to a Managed Services Provider that represents a BU inside a large product company. If this were a standalone MSP business, the accounting would likely be different.

Although MSP BUs are typically not directly responsible for hardware sales, hardware revenue and cost is included in Deal P&Ls in order to depict a holistic view of deal profitability. Therefore, how quickly and efficiently hardware is installed matters from a Deal P&L reporting standpoint. The quicker the hardware is installed and operational, the sooner the corresponding revenue and cost will be reflected in the (pro-forma) Deal P&L. So, when we talk about managing hardware revenue levers, we're really talking about ways to minimize the amount of time between when hardware is received and installed. In other words, tear down barriers that may exist. That said, let's talk about the most common barriers and what the delivery manager can do to take down those barriers. First, we will talk about a couple of externally controlled barrier examples, followed by a couple of internally controlled barriers.

One of the more significant externally controlled barriers is end-client site readiness. That is to say, there could be numerous reasons why a customer site is not ready to install hardware that has been received. Even with extensive pre-planning, there is always a risk the client site will not be ready. One of the keys to success is working closely and cooperatively with the designated client interface. And, if things are not progressing as planned, my advice is to escalate the matter, the sooner the better. Patiently waiting and hoping for behavior change on the part of a non-cooperative client interface is not a sensible strategy. The most effective countermeasure, along with the client interface, develop an activity-based project plan and make sure to remain on schedule via weekly status update meetings. Beyond that, you're basically at your client's mercy, since they essentially control what happens in their physical environment. In which case, diplomacy will always serve you better in situations you have little to no direct control. In other words, be as forceful and direct as you need to be, but do it in a reasonable and respectable manner. Working cooperatively with the client interface will always produce better results than being adversarial.

Another significant externally controlled barrier, which I have seen play out time and again, pertains to decentralized clients that have independently managed Business Units. In this case, I'm talking about *real* independence. As in headquarters (HQ) having little to no control over the BU executive managers. Even though there is a known potential risk, MPS deals are typically sold at the client HQ level, regardless of whether the company has a centralized or decentralized management structure. Generally speaking, the issues and challenges an MSP will face with centrally managed client companies are relatively few. Whereas, the opposite is often true when dealing with decentralized client companies. Why, you might be wondering? In the latter situation, HQ typically has little to no authority over BU management. Hence, even though the MSP Sales Team worked long and hard to sell the solution to the client's HQ management, they are potentially faced with having to re-sell it over and over again to each of the individual BU executive managers. The end result, implementation typically slows down to a crawl pace. And, if a BU executive is not sold on the benefits of the HQ sold solution, they may very well opt out of the deal.

So, what can a delivery or client manager do to improve this matter? The answer is very little, since the damage was done during the selling process. All you can realistically do in these undesirable situations is work like heck along with the Sales team to promote the merits of the solution to the resisting BU executives. If that does not work, my recommendation is given up trying to sell to uninterested executives, because at that point you are doing nothing more than wasting precious time and cycles.

One of the more significant internally controlled barriers is funding hardware leases. As mentioned earlier, for MPS (pro-forma) Deal P&L reporting purposes, hardware revenue is generally not recognized until the equipment is installed and operational. There are a series of chronological events that have to take place before leased hardware is funded and revenue can be recognized. Some of those events are physical activities, for example, product installation and activation. Many other events are administrative activities that have to be performed by various people involved in the hardware funding process. Those individuals typically include the delivery manager, transition manager, someone from Customer Admin, and someone from

Leasing Admin. There are a number of issues and challenges that can occur throughout the hardware funding process, which can potentially delay revenue recognition. In order to minimize processing delays, the delivery manager must closely monitor the entire funding process, and do everything reasonably possible to untangle any issues that may arise. Otherwise, received hardware can remain in limbo status for an extended period of time, which will of course result in revenue recognition delays.

Another significant internally controlled barrier has to do with distribution of product that is on allocation. In other words, product for which there is more demand than available supply. In these situations, diplomacy and making a sensible amount of noise usually works best. On the other hand, being obnoxious and making too much noise will usually backfire. Bottom line, if you want your client to get some of the allocated hardware, you must do everything reasonably possible to demonstrate why your client's needs are critical. Be reasonable and sensible about the amount of product you request. For example, settle for taking a few critical units now and postpone what you can for later delivery. Also, when there is an opportunity to do so, consider substituting with suitable alternative product. This kind of cooperation will not only help with your immediate needs, it will also go a long way helping you negotiate similar future needs. In dire product availability situations, the only way everyone wins is with a reasonable and balanced give and take approach. With regard to (pro-forma) Deal P&L impact, product allocation will almost certainly have an adverse effect, at least temporarily. Therefore, the more allocated product you can get committed to your deal, the more favorable the impact on your (pro-forma) Deal P&L.

With regard to hardware cost drivers, with one notable exception, there is little that can be done to influence cost, simply because hardware cost absolutely follows revenue. The exception I am referring has to do with Utility deals. Briefly, Utility deals are called that because they work like utility billing for metered electricity or natural gas that comes into your home. Just as your home utility company does not charge you for the cable and piping infrastructure, Managed Services Providers do not charge clients for the hardware and supplies used in MPS Utility deals. Instead, they simply charge for actual printed pages, based on contractually agreed price/page. Therefore, from a hardware cost standpoint, it behooves the MSP to utilize the most cost-effective hardware possible in Utility deals.

I'd like to discuss the unique aspects of Utility deal solutions in a little more detail. As with most everything else in business, there are hardly any *one size fits all* solutions. In an MPS solution, what might be an optimal printer model for a particular client location may be just the opposite for a different location. Let's assume we are in the process of placing printers in two very different client locations. One, in the Accounting Department, which is expected to print 10,000 pages/month. And the other, in the Legal Department, which is expected to print 50,000 pages/month. All things considered, let's assume optimal cost/page in the Accounting environment would be achieved using a $750 laser printer, which has a maximum duty cycle of 25,000 pages/month. Whereas, optimal cost/page in the Legal environment would be using a $2,500 laser printer, which has a maximum duty cycle of 100,000 pages/month. To be clear, cost/page is very different than price/page. The latter represents the price clients are charged for actual printed pages, while the former represents the MSP's cost of printing those pages. That said, if we were to switch those two printers between the Accounting and Legal Department, the MSP cost/page would be greater in both situations. Why? Because neither would represent an optimal printer model for those locations. Meanwhile, the client price/page remains unchanged, regardless of what printer models the MSP places in the client's environment. Bottom line, from a cost and profitability perspective, placement of optimal printer model matters.

In a real-life situation, the problem of having the wrong model printer in the wrong location generally occurs for one of two reasons. First, it could simply be due to a bad solution design. In other words, the wrong model printer was designated for a given location. The other reason, the actual number of pages printed on a given device turns out to be significantly different (usually lower) than the planned solution. The latter sometimes occurs because the requirements provided by the client were inaccurate. In other cases, it may be due to a change in the client's environment, which occurred after the solution design was completed. In yet other cases, it may be due to the client reducing their human resource or spinning off a business unit. Whatever the reason, it's the MSP that has to fix the problem because they own the entire cost of a Utility deal. Under the given circumstances, the MSP will likely attempt to swap out impacted printers in order to lower their cost. However, it's not as simple as it sounds. Before taking action, they must consider all of the costs associated with physically swapping out hardware units to ensure those actions will truly result in lower deal support cost. Otherwise, the lesser of two evils might be to leave the inappropriately placed printers where they are until a more cost-effective swapping opportunity presents itself.

At this point, I'd like to start talking about supplies revenue and cost levers. Unlike hardware and service, which are common components in virtually all Managed Services deals, supplies are consumption-based component that are unique to MPS deals. That said, there are a number of levers that can affect supplies revenue and cost, which we will discuss, starting with revenue levers.

Let's start with non-reporting print devices. These are devices that are not reporting printed pages, which is a foundational client billing requirement. Since printed pages are not being reported, the MSP is not generating any revenue from those devices. The fundamental problem, those printers are *not* linked to the network used by the MSP to collect printed page information. Hence, they are considered *blind* devices, which the MSP is basically servicing and supporting for free. Great deal for the client, but not so good for the MSP.

Aside from using a tedious and costly manual meter reading process, it's only through a network connection that printed page information is collected and billed to the client. Incidentally, this type of problem does not typically occur in small client environments, which tend to remain relatively static. However, it does occur in large client buildings and campus environments. The primary reason, those environments are often in a constant state of flux, which means losing sight of some printers that are not connected to the network is entirely possible. In these situations, it is particularly important for the MSP to pay special attention to any charges that occur in the client's environment, which can be accomplished a couple of different ways. First, do periodic physical inventory and/or routine spot checks of the hardware in the client's environment. The second way is through consumption reporting analysis.

Generally speaking, the MSP will have analytical reporting tools available, which show such things as number of pages billed versus toner consumption, at both the device and total client level. It's through this type of analysis the MSP can identify *red flags,* and proceed to resolve noted problems. Incidentally, even with these countermeasures, there is always the possibility a few stragglers will slip through the cracks. Nevertheless, a reasonable amount of routine due diligence and data analysis will always serve you best.

Another common supplies revenue problem occurs when toner is shipped to a client for non-entitled devices. In other words, devices that are not covered under the MPS contract. Here again, this type of problem is more common in large client environments where they are more likely to have identical printer models, with some covered under contract and others not covered. The reason this is a potential problem, its commonplace to have the same on-site resource support both contracted and non-contracted printers in the client environment. Although it's becoming increasingly common for customers to utilize the automated toner replacement feature, which is configurable in the printer software, a considerable number of customers do not use that feature. Instead, they order replacement toner the old-fashioned way, by calling the MSP Customer Service Center (CSC).

Therein lies the problem. The reason being, unless devices are clearly marked, and the markings are acknowledged by the on-site support resource, all the printers in the client's environment are treated the same way. Meaning, when a printer is running low on toner, the on-site resource simply calls the MSP CSC for a replacement toner. If the CSC does not have a reliable entitlement verification process in place, *including model/serial number validation,* guess what happens? The CSC administrator will ask the on-site resource for a contract number and printer model number. Since the client has several of that particular model printer in their environment (some under contract and some not), a replacement toner is shipped to the client with no further questions asked. Instead, the CSC Administrator should also be validating the printer serial number. Omitting that last step results in shipping free toner to the client. Incidentally, toner is the single most profitable aspect of servicing and supporting printer products.

By the way, I am not suggesting these are deliberate actions on the part of the client to avoid paying for replacement toner. In large campus environments, the on-site support resource calling for toner replacement may not be aware of which devices are under contract and which are not. That individual is usually only interested in one thing, having the printers in the environment in continuous working order, which brings us to the following obvious conclusion. Under *all* circumstances, contract entitlement verification must include both model and serial number validation. Otherwise, the MSP bottom line will suffer the consequences.

Now let's talk about supplies cost improvement levers. Compared to what can be done to positively impact supplies revenue, there are abundantly more cost levers available that can impact profitability. Let's start with one of the more significant impact items, recording toner cost. Since it's virtually impossible to absolutely match supplies revenue with cost, Managed Services Providers are forced to use a practical yet imperfect accounting method to record toner cost. In a perfect world, each month end, supplies cost would be recorded based on actual toner consumed for billed printed pages that month. The fact of the matter, getting down to that level of detail would require a significant amount of unjustifiable effort, and result in only marginally more accurate Deal P&Ls.

Therefore, the second best method is to simply record the entire cost of the toner cartridge when it's shipped to the client. With one notable exception, we are dealing with a relatively negligible revenue vs. cost timing issue, specifically, actual consumption timing. The exception being, toner that is shipped and stocked at client sites. As mentioned earlier, stocked toner is intended to be a countermeasure for availability challenges that sometimes occur during the hardware deployment phase. After deployment is completed, toner is generally shipped to the client on a just-in-time basis, triggered by the automated re-order feature in the printer software.

Unfortunately, what starts out as a well-intentioned countermeasure will often gradually turn into an out-of-control situation. That is to say, it will result in long forgotten toner inventory sitting idle inside some client back room or closet. Incidentally, even though I am referring to the extra toner as inventory, from an accounting standpoint, all shipped toner would have already been charged to cost of sales on the Deal P&L, which realistically represents an extraordinary deal cost burden.

For those of you who are accounting minded, you might be asking yourself, why aren't those extra toners treated as consigned inventory? Under different circumstances, that would certainly be an acceptable accounting treatment. However, for Managed Print Services deals, it's important to remember the MSP is providing a service. Basically, that means the client couldn't care less about how toner is managed, as long as contracted service deliverables are met or exceeded. Furthermore, it's simply unreasonable to expect the client to agree to normal consignment terms, which would hold them financially accountable for the inventory. In which case, consignment is basically off the table. Leaving only one viable accounting option, which is treating shipped toner as cost of sales. Therefore, it behooves the MSP to do everything reasonably possible to minimize the amount of toner stored at customer sites, and credit cost of sales for toner brought back in-house.

Correcting an out-of-control toner inventory situation like the one described can be quite cumbersome and costly. Also, those situations oftentimes require cooperation and assistance from the client, which does not always come easy. First, you have to identify the multiple back rooms and closets where toner may be stored, which will be challenging to say the least. Then you have to count and catalog the toner items. Finally, you have to develop a return and/or consumption strategy, meaning determine the most economically sensible way of dealing with those toner cartridges. The fact of the matter, the aftermath of poorly managed initial toner provisioning can turn into a challenging cost problem. Therefore, the best way to avoid the problem in the first place is by doing a good job managing and controlling inventory that is located at client sites.

Another significant supplies cost improvement lever is related to toner threshold management. Simply put, that means maximizing the amount of toner yield. So, how do you actually do that? Set the automated toner re-order point to a reasonably low level, ensuring essentially all of the powder in the toner cartridge is consumed. Typically, you can consume 95% or more of the powder inside a cartridge before you start noticing an ever-so-slight print quality degradation. In most work environments, there is no problem setting the alert at 5% toner remaining. It's only in highly visible environments, such as a client executive suite, you may want to consider setting the re-order point moderately above 5% remaining. Otherwise, having the re-order point at, let's say, 10, 15, or 20% toner remaining is a complete waste of money.

Surprisingly, in many poorly managed environments the re-order point is automatically set at those ridiculously high levels. Setting a more reasonable re-order point is something the delivery manager can easily and effectively control via automated tools build into the printer software. Remember, printing is all about ink (or toner) cost. Therefore, the better you manage ink consumption, the more profitable will be your MPS business. Although there are a number of other supplies cost management levers we could discuss, I'm going to stop here and assume you get the general idea. Bottom line, it behooves the MSP to continuously perform basic reasonableness tests, such as comparing printed pages to toner consumption, as well as utilize cost effective processes and guidelines to optimally manage supplies inventory and consumption.

Finally, let's talk about service revenue and cost levers, once again starting with revenue. Unlike supplies, which is a consumption-based component of MPS deals, service is a principal component in all Managed Services deal types. That said, one of the fundamental principles of service billing is, the actual service level delivered must correspond with the amount clients are billed. Delivering materially higher or lower than contracted service level is equally bad for business, from both a revenue and cost standpoint. For now, we will focus on revenue implications of over and under delivering, and later we will talk about cost implications.

There are two distinct ways over-delivery normally occurs. One way, the MSP consistently delivers above contracted service levels. In other words, if the contracted service level is to achieve 95% service incident resolution within eight hours, consistently achieving 98% represents over-delivery. Although consistent over-delivery may be viewed favorably by the client, it's clearly an unnecessary cost and/or lost revenue opportunity for the MSP. If the client truly wants or needs 98% performance, they should be billed for the higher service level. The other way over-delivery occurs is when customer concessions are allowed, meaning not billing for the extra work the client has requested. It's okay to allow clients occasional concessions. As a matter of fact, I personally believe it's good business, but only to a point. Even though concession is a dirty word in business, it's often viewed as a cost of doing business. That is particularly true for long-term contracts like Managed Services deals, which a reasonable amount of cooperative give and take will almost always result in better client/vendor relationship.

On the other hand, if you allow your client to push you around, demanding more and more concessions for the privilege of doing business with them, you have lost control. And more importantly, you probably also lost your client's respect. If you haven't experienced this first hand, allow me to digress for a moment to explain how concessions play a role in normal and healthy business to business relationships.

Once a lengthy and detailed service contract is signed, most customers want to be able to place that document on the shelf and refer to it *only* when it's absolutely necessary. If the delivery or client manager is constantly waving the service contract in front of the client, pointing out what's included and excluded from the agreement, the client will surely become increasingly frustrated. Consequently, instead of gaining an ally and potentially a good reference account, which is valued like gold in business, you will almost certainly create an adversarial relationship with your client.

By the way, no reasonable client is going to expect most everything they request over and above contracted deliverables to be done for free. As usual, the best solution is finding that sensible middle ground where both parties give a little to get a little. Bottom line, aside from a reasonable number of customer satisfaction concessions, the delivery or client manager must make sure the client is billed for services rendered. The best way to ensure that's done is to present the client with a Charge Order whenever they request relatively significant out-of-scope services. Let the small stuff go, which most customers will appreciate and likely pay dividends in the future, in terms of expanded and/or new business opportunities.

Another manageable service revenue lever in MPS deals is making sure to identify and bill non-reporting devices for similar reasons stated above in the supplies levers section. As mentioned earlier, non-reporting (or network blind) devices means you are losing supplies revenue resulting from unbilled printed pages. Likewise, network blind devices also result in lost service revenue. Hence, there is double incentive for the delivery manager to identify and add those non-reporting devices to the network.

Now let's move on to service cost improvement levers. Just as with supplies, there are abundantly more service cost levers than revenue levers that can be managed to improve profitability. Here again, I do not intend to discuss all those details, but I will talk about a few of the more significant impact levers. Let's start with a common one, over-delivering contracted service levels (SLAs). Earlier, we talked about the fact that over-delivering SLAs adversely impacts revenue. I briefly mentioned it does the same to cost. In the Managed Services world, when one refers to over-delivery, the first thing that comes to mind is the services provider is incurring more delivery cost than is otherwise necessary. Thus, if you are trying to preserve or improve the bottom line, it's advisable to keep your delivery cost in line with contracted services deliverables.

A Managed Services contractual agreement represents the culmination of a negotiated deal between the client and MSP. Once finalized, the contract is managed by humans who sit on opposite sides of the table and naturally have opposing allegiances. Over time, as professional relationships are developed and nurtured, people from both sides typically start loosening up and work more cooperatively with one another. Meaning both parties will bend a little without disputing relatively insignificant contract terms and deliverables. However, one must be careful not to bend too far, especially the service provider. Generally speaking, it's the MSP that bends more than the client in these contractual relationships, often resulting in over-delivering SLAs.

In an ideal situation, the service provider would want to moderately over-deliver for client satisfaction reasons. On the other hand, excessive over-delivery is simply not necessary and will certainly adversely impact deal profitability. Bottom line, overcompensating one way or the other is simply not good business. In which case, being overly petty and constantly waving the signed contract in front of your client is not advisable. Just as it is not advisable to bend over backwards for your client, while incurring totally unnecessary support cost. Staying within a reasonable and respectful middle ground will always serve you best, from both a relationship and profitability standpoint.

Generally speaking, there are three significant cost categories the delivery manager can control in MPS deals, including: resource cost, break/fix cost, and third-party cost. These three categories typically make up the lion's share of total deal service and support cost. Hence, we are going to talk about each of them in more detail, along with managing related levers and knobs that can potentially improve deal profitability.

Most Managed Services organizations utilize three different types of resource cost centers, including those for: management and overhead resources, dedicated deal resources, and shared resources. Let's get the two easy ones out of the way. First, management and overhead cost centers are used for resources that essentially have nothing directly to do with supporting contracted deals. Therefore, at the end of each month, those costs are usually allocated to Deal P&Ls based on percentage of total revenue or total cost. Second, we already talked about dedicated resources who are directly coded to deal cost centers, making their cost capture for Deal P&L reporting relatively easy and straightforward. That leaves us with the third category, namely, shared resource cost.

The way shared resource cost is funneled into Deal P&Ls is typically via a Labor Tracking & Costing system, which is utilized by shared resources to charge labor cost to deals they support. We already had a fairly lengthy discussion regarding Labor Tracking and Costing systems in Chapter 5. Therefore, I will simply reiterate that reports generated from those systems are critically important, and should routinely be reviewed by delivery managers for two reasons. First, validate legitimate shared resource cost has been charged to their deal, and challenge any charges that appear to have been erroneously posted against their deal. Intentional or not, reporting errors occur. And when they do, you need to identify and correct them in order to preserve the financial health of your deal.

The second reason Labor Tracking & Costing system reports are important is they can be used by delivery managers to assess whether or not they are spending money wisely. For example, let's assume you are utilizing shared transition managers to get your deal up and running. Normally, transition managers can either work from customer sites, which is common for complex deals and large campus environments, or work remotely. Relatively speaking, remote transition managers are typically lower cost resources. Furthermore, they do not incur travel cost, which can be significant for on-site transition managers.

In any case, when you review the shared labor report, you suddenly realize most of the transition managers supporting your deal are on-site resources. Given your deal has been in transition phase for a few months with several more months to go, you conclude much of the challenging work that required on-site resources is now completed. Moreover, you determine at least half of the remaining work can be done by remote transition resources. So, you set up a meeting with the Transition Department Manager and agree on making a resource distribution adjustment, which ends up saving your deal tens of thousands of dollars each month. On the other hand, if a delivery manager is too busy to bother looking at shared resource cost reports, savings like we just discussed would not be realized. Hence, the Deal P&L suffers the resulting consequences.

Next, let's talk about managing break/fix cost levers. But first, I'd like to discuss the sources of break/fix support, which typically come from one or more of the following. First, an internal Service & Support organization whose principal responsibility is to provide warranty and billable contract support for the company's products. Second, an internal break/fix organization that is dedicated to supporting MPS deals. And third, external break/fix vendors who are hired to either exclusively provide on-site support, or augment internal support capabilities. In large technology product companies that also have Managed Services offerings, break/fix support is generally provided by the internal Service & Support organization. Leveraging a single internal infrastructure to support both independently sold product, as well as product embedded into Managed Services deals, usually makes more economic sense. On the other hand, when internal break/fix organizations do not exist, support for Managed Services deals is limited to the other two above mentioned sources.

Now let's talk about those three break/fix options in more detail, starting with vendor support. Leveraging independent regional, national, or global on-site support vendors is inherently risky from a service quality standpoint. Furthermore, they typically require a considerable amount of oversight by the MSP that is utilizing their services. A best-case scenario is utilizing a single third-party vendor that covers the entire geography the MSP has clients. Let me explain why that is. Service and support vendors are typically utilized by an MSP in one of two ways. The first way, to support a single client that has sites located throughout a given region. In this case, the MSP would ideally want a vendor that covers that entire client geography. The primary reason, achieving consistent service quality from multiple vendors is often difficult, if not impossible. As a matter of fact, I can almost guarantee there will be quality management challenges in those situations. Clients expect and deserve to receive consistent service quality, no matter how big or small the geography they operate.

The second way, an MSP might utilize a service vendor is to support multiple clients located across an entire region, for example the USA. For the very same reason given in the first scenario (achieving consistent service quality), the MSP's best bet is utilizing a single vendor that covers the entire nation. Despite the fact what I just suggested would be considered ideal, it is often challenging for an MSP to find an ideal vendor support solution. Meaning, they may have to utilize multiple vendors to cover the entire geography their clients are located. Accordingly, quality management issues are sure to arise from time to time. My point being, no matter the situation, the fewer on-site support vendors the MSP utilizes, the more manageable will be controlling service quality.

Generally speaking, from an economic standpoint, the least desirable option is setting up an independent break/fix organization just to support Managed Services deals. In which case, the size of the Managed Services business matters. The smaller the business, the less likely this option will make economic sense. On-site service is all about coverage. Having satisfactory geographic coverage, which does not require a significant amount of travel time and cost to go from one customer site to another, is an essential component of an efficient service delivery model. In service businesses, travel represents nothing more than consumption of what could otherwise be productive time, coupled with accompanying travel cost. The more travel required, the less productive time will be available, and the greater will be overall service and support cost. Bottom line, an independent Managed Services break/fix organization is only justifiable when the overall business size is significant and/or customers are concentrated in limited physical locations such as major cities or large campus sites. If clients are thinly spread throughout a large region or country, having an independent Managed Services break/fix organization simply does not make economic sense.

Oftentimes, a combination of two of the three above mentioned break/fix support solutions is utilized. For example, let's assume you're an MSP with roughly 50% of your customer installed base located in a dozen major cities and an equal number of major campus sites, and the remaining installed base is widespread throughout the nation in relatively small sites. A blended solution utilizing dedicated Managed Services beak/fix resources in major cities and campus sites, and vendor support for smaller remote sites would likely make the most economic sense. The same would hold true if you had access to an internal Service & Support organization that could team up with service vendors to provide a blended solution. I will tell you from personal experience, with proper planning and good vendor management practices, blended on-site service delivery solutions have often proven to be worthwhile and cost effective. They just require a little extra management oversight.

In addition to making the best break/fix delivery option, there are other on-site support cost levers delivery managers can leverage. For example, let's assume you are a delivery manager responsible for an MPS deal that your company's internal product support organization is providing on-site service. In that case, you're likely receiving a monthly report showing all the dispatched on-site calls for your deal, including hours worked, parts used, etc. Let's assume further, based on a glance at the report totals, the monthly charge appears to be in the expected ballpark. The total number of dispatched calls, as well as total labor and parts cost is roughly in line with what would be expected for your deal size and scope. With report in hand, you have two choices you can make. One, accept the fact the report totals are correct, and don't bother looking further into the details for cost improvement opportunities. In other words, do what many other delivery managers would do, which is to simply cast the report aside. After all, you can't be bothered looking at minutia level details when you have so many more important things to do. Yes, I'm being sarcastic.

The other option is actually taking a close look at the report details. You may be surprised at what you find. It's only by exercising the second option that you suddenly realize the following. During the past three months, five out of 100 hardware units in your client's environment accounted for approximately 50% of the service incidents. As a matter of fact, when you look at the labor and parts cost for servicing those five hardware units during the past three months, you suddenly realize the aggregate service cost is actually greater than the hardware replacement cost. This example may sound a little extreme to you. Trust me, things like this really do happen. It's not unusual for a few *lemon* products in a given environment to be responsible for the lion's share of on-site service incidents. Meanwhile, the remaining products keep running with virtually no required remedial service.

Incidentally, I mention remedial service because I am a firm believer that routine preventative maintenance should never be ignored. There are endless proven examples demonstrating why doing so is shortsighted and consequential. In any case, let's get back to those five *lemons* in the environment. Now that you (the delivery manager) has been empowered with useful information, the next logical step is to replace those five hardware units with more reliable problem-free products. By the way, the scenario we just discussed is not just a deal cost issue. As you might imagine, customers are not happy when hardware repeatedly fails in their environment, which means you also have a customer satisfaction issue on your hands.

Now, let's talk about how to manage third-party vendor cost levers. To be clear, we are talking about a broader category of third-party vendors, not just on-site service providers. MSP organizations are likely to utilize third party vendors for a number of different reasons. For example, they might bring contracted workers on board to address temporary work spikes. They may bring in a specialty resource who possesses skills that are not available internally. The latter is most commonly used for time-defined short and medium term projects. However, there are situations in which a specialty resource might be brought on board for a longer undefined period, meaning remain on board as long as there are meaningful and worthwhile projects for that resource to address.

In other situations, an MSP might engage with a third-party vendor to gain access to low-cost near-shore or offshore resources that provide routine end-client Customer Service and/or Technical Support. An MSP might also seek vendor resources to augment a broad range of other activities such as: discovery, transition, deployment, and steady state support. Whatever the reason for engaging with third party vendors, from a cost management standpoint the same basic principles apply. First and foremost, the MSP must continually re-evaluate cost versus value. The reason being, in a fluid and dynamic business like Managed Services, the need for vendor supplied resources constantly change. Meaning, as business conditions and/or deal life cycle phase change, so too may change the need for vendor resources.

Whenever you find yourself approaching the tipping point in terms of cost versus value, it's time to take action. That may mean seeking a lower cost vendor, or possibly requesting a lower price from an existing vendor. From personal experience, I will tell you the latter is not as uncommon as you might otherwise imagine, particularly during unusually difficult business circumstances. Depending on other choices your vendor has, their best option may be to continue doing business with you at a lower price rather than losing your business. Simply put, you won't know unless you ask. Some vendors subscribe to the following notion. Stick with your client during the thick and thin, and they will reciprocate by rewarding you with additional business in the future. On the other hand, if your existing vendor refuses to budge on price, the only other viable option you may have is changing vendors. However, allow me to offer a word of caution here. Depending on the complexity of the services the existing vendor provides, this option requires careful evaluation of all related impact items before a vendor changeover decision is actually made. Otherwise, what may appear to be worthwhile on the surface could turn out to be consequential for both you (the MSP) and your end-clients.

And finally, another example of a third-party vendor cost lever relates to something we discussed earlier. Specifically, making sure your vendor is accountable for the same service level deliverables you (the MSP) is accountable to your end-client. In other words, if you are contractually obligated to provide your client with, let's say, 98% same day incident resolution, your third-party vendor should be held accountable for the same performance level. Otherwise, the financial implications of missed end-client deliverables rests totally on your shoulders. Meaning, you will be responsible for any applicable non-performance penalties, while your vendor continues to get paid for delivering relatively low-level service quality. As obvious as that issue may appear to be, you would be surprised how often contract language between the MSP and vendor do not address end-client deliverables. Bottom line, whenever third party vendors are involved, it's always best to have three-way contractual alignment regarding service level performance between you (the MSP), your client, and your third-party vendor. Otherwise, the risk associated with poor service delivery performance will rest totally on your shoulders.

Although there are several other vendor cost control levers available, the last one we will discuss is ensuring vendor invoices are always reviewed and validated for accuracy. I cannot tell you the countless times I found errors in vendor invoices. Incidentally, that's only the first step in the problem resolution process. The next two steps include bringing the error to the vendor's attention, and subsequently ensuring a credit is processed for the erroneous billing. Invoicing errors can occur for a number of different reasons, regardless of whether they are systematically generated or created from manual input into a billing system. However, I can safely state that, for the most part invoicing errors are unintentional.

The fact of the matter, mistakes happen in business just as they do elsewhere. A best practice I've seen work very effectively is having the vendor issue preliminary invoices, and allowing the MSP sufficient time to review and approve those invoices before they are finally issued. On the surface, this extra step may appear to be cumbersome and unnecessary. Trust me, it's less cumbersome than having to issue credits for invoicing errors, which incidentally does not bode well for client/vendor relationships. In order for this process to work effectively, there needs to be reasonable timeframe restrictions placed on the review process. For example, allow the MSP, let's say, a maximum of 5 days to review and approve the preliminary invoices. A longer grace period would likely contribute to invoice payment delays, which will of course adversely affect the vendor's cash flow. Bottom line, there needs to be strict guidelines wrapped around this process in order for it to work effectively.

There is one last item I'd like to discuss before leaving the subject of levers and knobs. In most Managed Services solutions that include hardware, whether it's computing, printing, or any other type of equipment, the hardware is usually leased. Furthermore, instead of being directly leased to the end-client, the hardware is generally leased to the MSP and subsequently indirectly billed to the end-client via a bundled solution price. The intent is to have the MSP fully recover the pass-through leasing cost from the end-client via the bundled billing. However, the monthly leasing cost and billing amount almost never exactly match. The resulting variance between the two values is referred to as Embedded Lease Variance (ELV), which has to be reflected somewhere on the MSP Deal P&L. Although ELV could be positive, most times it's negative. In which case, for P&L reporting purposes, it's treated as contra-revenue. Simply put, contra-revenue impacts the P&L much like a customer credit does, effectively lowering earned revenue.

One of the predominant reasons ELV ends up being negative is the Deal Solution team will often bake into the solution financials the most optimistic volume assumptions possible. For example, in an MPS utility deal they will assume a higher printed page volume than could realistically be achieved. In doing so, the hardware leasing component of per page bundled billing price is lower than it should rightfully be.

Allow me to explain why these bogus assumptions have a negative impact on ELV. Lease billing to the lessee (MSP in this case) represents a fixed cost, whereas, consumption-based billing to the client represents variable revenue. Hence, the higher the consumption volume, the higher the aggregate lease billing to the client. The fact of the matter, this deal solution pricing strategy generally ends up being nothing more than wishful planning, resulting in the MSP being stuck with long-term recurring negative ELV. It's only after the deal is won and the solution is rolled out that everyone else (besides the Deal Solution team) suddenly realize those unrealistic volumes will never materialize. Bottom line, since the client indirectly pays for hardware leasing via consumption based bundled billing, the lower the actual print volume, the lower will be the aggregate lease billing, which means the higher will be the negative ELV.

Given these and other hardware lease management challenges, what can you realistically do to leverage available levers and knobs? The answer is plenty, including the following two notable actions. First and foremost, compare the detailed lease billing report provided by the financing organization to the end-client detailed billing report. You may find leasing charges for hardware units that are not included in your deal. Humans are responsible for setting up leasing schedules, and humans make mistakes. It's your job as deal account manager to find those mistakes and have them rectified.

Second, you might find charges in the leasing report for defective hardware units you thought were long returned, which no one ever actually contacted the leasing company to request return authorizations. The leasing company has no problem accommodating these oversights. The fact that you or someone else on your account management team may be dragging your heels or forgotten about those defective units does not concern the leasing company in the least. Reconciling reports is mundane work that some people are simply not willing to do, especially when they have other more important (or should we say more pleasant) things to do with their limited available time. But, here is the reality of the situation. In most circumstances, the return value generated from scrubbing business critical reports is almost guaranteed to exceed scrubbing cost. The lesson here is to pay attention to all of the business critical reports that are made available to your account management team. You are likely to find something worthwhile in those reports, which would otherwise have gone unnoticed.

Increasing Deal Size and Scope

Now that we've discussed the various aspects of Actual Deal P&L management in a fair amount of detail, there is one other related item I'd like to address, namely, increasing deal size and scope. Although profitability is and always will be the most important aspect of P&L management, growing the top line also matters. Therefore, we're going to talk briefly about the deal manager's selling responsibilities. In this case, I am referring to the delivery and/or client manager. In small, medium and moderately large deals, the delivery manager is typically responsible for all aspects of account management, including owning the Deal P&L and increasing the deal scope and size. Whereas, in very large and strategic deals, the client manager (an added oversight resource) is typically responsible for those things. In other words, the client manager assumes the account team leader role, while the delivery manager is relegated to a subordinate role overseeing day-to-day account operations activities.

In most Managed Services businesses, the Sales organization is responsible for selling new and renewal deals. Whereas, the Deal P&L owner is responsible for increasing existing deal scope and size, which is generally handled through the so-called Change Order process. That means those managers must constantly keep their eyes and ears opened for expanded business opportunities, which could present themselves in a number of different ways. It could be an opportunity to expand an existing solution to another business unit within the client's business. It could be an opportunity to sell a software solution that improves the client's productivity. Or it could simply be a request from the client to deliver more or higher-level services. Remember, business-savvy clients know how to effectively get more for less or no additional cost. Regardless of how business-savvy your client may be, it's your responsibility as Deal P&L owner to present them with a billable Change Order whenever it is deemed appropriate and necessary. However, it's also important to be mindful that nitpicking is not smart. Meaning it's not wise to stick a Charge Order under your client's nose every time they ask for the slightest thing not covered under the contract. On the other hand, neither is giving away what could otherwise represent relatively significant incremental revenue.

Incidentally, under normal circumstances, profit generated from Change Orders is typically higher than profit generated from in-scope contracted work. Hence, Change Orders are very important from a margin contribution perspective. Bottom line, don't be overly aggressive or apprehensive presenting your client with Change Orders. As a matter of fact, I recommend establishing guidelines for your delivery and client managers to help them decide when a Charge Order is deemed appropriate. If you leave it up to the individual account managers without guidelines, you will likely experience a wide range of inconsistencies. That means clients who are given extra leeway will be happy, while clients who are *not* given a reasonable amount of leeway will surely be unhappy, which could result in undesirable future problems and challenges with those clients.

Chapter 10

Managing Forecast Deal P&Ls

Generally speaking, forecasting is as much an art form as it is a science; whereby, accuracy and reliability improves with training and experience. The science is making probability assumptions regarding pipeline and anticipated future orders, as well as leveraging historical performance data to establish a recurring revenue and cost baseline associated with the installed base. To ensure baseline revenue and cost are accurate, anomalies must be identified and removed from historical financial data. Furthermore, consideration must be given to external environmental factors that could affect your client's business or industry, as well as any applicable seasonality factors.

There are two distinct types of seasonality factors that could affect the forecast. First, seasonality in the service provider's business. That is to say, typical high and low volume months in the MSP's business. Second, the seasonality in the client's business, which is especially important for the recurring portion of the Deal P&L forecast. For example, if your client is an Accounting firm, you would likely consider a volume spike during the March/April timeframe, when demand for tax preparation and filing typically peaks. On the other hand, if your client is a retailer, you would likely consider a spike at the end of the calendar year, when retail business typically peaks.

Beyond the items just mentioned, there are other factors that must be considered when creating an MPS Deal P&L forecast. One of those is the so-called *hardware conversion factor*. In other words, the amount of time it takes from when the hardware is shipped until it becomes operational at the client's site. The projected time frame is important for two reasons. First, as mentioned earlier, for (pro-forma) Deal P&L reporting purposes, hardware revenue and cost are generally not recognized until the devices are operational. Second, the recurring revenue and cost associated with services and any applicable consumables (such as printer toner) will not take effect until the hardware devices become operational.

Another item that must be considered in an MPS Deal P&L forecast is the contract life cycle phase. MPS deals have three distinct life cycle phases that usually form a standard bell curve. There is a gradual ramp-up in business volume during the deal deployment phase, which could vary from a few months up to a year or more in duration. Then there is a long steady state phase, in which relatively few if any changes are typically made to the deployed environment. And finally, there is a ramp-down phase as the deal approaches end of life, which could be as long and gradual as the deployment phase (in reverse). On the other hand, there are some contracts that abruptly end. The contract terms dictate how the ramp-down phase will be handled. In any event, the impact these life cycle phases have on a Deal P&L forecast can be fairly dramatic.

The art form of forecasting is applying learned skills to produce an accurate and clear view of future business outcome. By the way, some people naturally possess those skills, while others struggle with them. And, in some cases, they will never develop those skills. I realize that may sound somewhat cruel and insensitive. The fact of the matter, some people simply do not have the aptitude for forecasting. Accuracy and reliability are not just dependent on a person's learned forecasting skill. It also depends on the level of business acumen the forecaster possesses. Generally speaking, the greater the level of business acumen, the better quality and more reliable the forecasts are likely to be.

Contrary to common misbelief, at its core, forecasting is more so a business management than Finance responsibility. Forecasting can essentially be broken down into two categories: business forecasting and financial forecasting. Let's discuss financial forecasting first because it's relatively easier and more straightforward. For the most part, financial forecasts essentially represent aggregated or consolidated views of several business forecasts. For example, they could reflect a total region, country, or global view. Whereas, business forecasts are typically created by business managers and are much more granular, taking into account nitty-gritty details that affect the specific business or deal being forecasted.

The forecasting guidelines that a company or BU utilizes can have a major impact on forecasting accuracy and reliability. Most businesses utilize a rating scale to assign a probability level to new and expanded business opportunities in the sales funnel. There are a number of potential factors that could be considered when assigning a probability rating. I would say the probability assessment provided by the Sales Account Manager generally carries the most weight. As for actual forecasting guidelines, some companies may simply take the following position. Any new or expanded business opportunity that is assigned 50% or greater probability rating will be included in the forecast. Whereas, opportunities that are assigned a probability below 50% are excluded from the forecast. Other companies may use the assigned probability rating as a multiplier that is applied to the dollarized business opportunity. For example, a $50M deal with a 50 % probability rating will result in incorporating $25M in the forecast.

The given examples represent two of the most basic and common methodologies used. Nevertheless, companies will generally utilize whatever forecasting guidelines have historically produced the most reliable results. Ultimately, the one thing that matters most is forecasting accuracy, which represents a measurement of how close historical actuals have been to forecasts. Next, we will discuss the two major aspects of business forecasting, namely, process and tools.

Forecasting Process

As mentioned earlier, to a large extent forecasting is a learned skill. Unlike some other more straightforward business processes, forecasting is not something you can simply diagram a flowchart and tell someone to handle. One must also learn how to effectively use a forecasting tool, something we will discuss in more detail shortly. Furthermore, the individual must minimally possess foundational financial knowledge, starting with understanding the financial implications of business transactions. If the person creating the forecast does not understand how business transactions impact the company financials, it's hardly reasonable to expect that individual to produce dependable and reliable forecasts.

Equally important, the person creating the forecast must have a good understanding of business drivers. Meaning, when a specific business event occurs, what can reasonably be expected to follow and how long will it take for follow-on action to occur? For example, if your company ships a piece of hardware today, what would be a reasonable timeframe for that hardware to be installed and start generating annuity revenue? In some businesses it might be reasonable to assume immediately, while in other businesses it might be more reasonable to assume a month or more delay. In the latter case, the product might require software installation and testing at the client's site before the equipment is operational. This is just one example of the myriad of potential factors that might affect a forecast. In the real world, it's typically more complicated than just considering one basic factor like the one described. Furthermore, the complexity of the forecasting process generally goes hand and hand with the complexity of the business being forecasted.

On the easy end of the spectrum, forecasting, let's say, a material distribution business is relatively straightforward. In this case, you normally only take into account the timing and quantity of inputs and outputs. In other words, purchases you make from suppliers represent input, and sales made to your customers represent output. Hence, both the input and output streams can typically be well managed and controlled. That is to say, input is managed with Purchase Orders you issue to your suppliers, along with a material release schedule. And output is managed by projected customer shipments. Furthermore, in this type of business, large repetitive customers will often sign up to provide monthly demand forecasts, which will help you produce more reliable and accurate forecasts.

On the hard end of the spectrum, forecasting for an MPS business is unquestionably more challenging and more complicated than a distribution business. The reason being, MPS deals contain hardware, service, and supplies components. In which case, revenue and cost must be individually considered for each component. Furthermore, the behavior of each component, in terms of projected revenue and cost timing is different. Given the complexity of MPS deal forecasting, I'm going to spend a considerable amount of time discussing those details to give you an appreciation of the inherent challenges.

Let's start with hardware forecasting for an MPS deal, which incidentally also drives supplies and service annuity streams. The first thing you need to know about hardware is the company's revenue recognition policy. At this point, you might be thinking to yourself, what is there to know? You ship the hardware and recognize the corresponding revenue and cost upon shipment. Although that is the case for product businesses, it is typically not the case for MPS businesses. The fact of the matter, with potential insistence from external auditors, MPS businesses or BUs may have to adhere to more conservative revenue recognition policies. That is to say, adopt more restrictive revenue recognition guidelines regarding leased hardware that is embedded in MPS deals. The policy may state that hardware revenue and cost cannot be recognized until the unit is funded by the leasing entity. And, the pre-requisite for the lease funded is having the hardware unit installed and operational at the customer's site, as well as completing all of the corresponding paperwork which flows through multiple cross-functional organizations. In other unique contractual arrangements, the company may be required to recognize hardware revenue ratably over the entire life of the deal, which could be five years or more.

As you can see from the couple given examples, hardware revenue recognition is not necessarily a simple black and white matter. For the most part, a combination of internal company policy and accounting regulations dictate how revenue will be recognized under varying circumstances. These are precisely the types of things that need to be taken into account when creating an MPS deal hardware revenue forecast. By the way, once the revenue recognition process has been established, hardware cost forecasting is easy because it strictly follows revenue.

Although most MPS deals include a hardware component, that is not always the case. In deals that do not include hardware, the client either buys the hardware separately or they utilize pre-existing hardware. In either of those two cases, we would only concern ourselves with forecasting the recurring components of the deal, namely, supplies and services. However, from what I have observed, most clients buy solutions that include hardware, supplies, and services. And, in most of those cases, hardware is financed as embedded leases.

The two biggest challenges associated with MPS deals hardware forecasting are projecting: 1) when the hardware will ship, and 2) when it will be installed and operational. There are a couple of reasons why these two events are important. First, as mentioned earlier, it's not uncommon for a conservative company to hold off recognizing revenue until the hardware is installed and operational. Second, which was also mentioned earlier, hardware drives the annuity streams. Accordingly, in order for the Deal P&L owner to have a good handle on projected hardware shipments, he must work closely with product release personnel. In addition, he needs to work closely with the transition manager to forecast when the equipment will be installed and operational. That's the level of detail you must consider when determining how much hardware revenue and cost should be included in the MPS Deal P&L Forecast.

What oftentimes makes projecting hardware installation and operational dates challenging is customer site readiness issues, which the deal management team has virtually no control and typically little ability to influence. Every customer situation is different, with each having unique dependencies and challenges. With some customers, you can reasonably expect hardware to be operational within, let's say, one month after shipment. With other customers, you simply don't know. You may be waiting months for the hardware placement area to be ready. Likewise, you may be waiting for clients to work through internal issues that are preventing you from moving forward, which can sometimes be dreadfully slow. These are only a few examples of situations that can make projecting hardware installation and operational dates challenging. Unfortunately, with some customers, that's just the way it is. And, there is little, if anything, the P&L owner can do about it, making forecasting that much more challenging.

Although there are challenges associated with forecasting hardware, forecasting supplies and service revenue and cost typically present even bigger challenges. We will get into the details shortly, first supplies followed by services. Before we start talking about supplies forecasting, I'd like to point out that there are a number of different billing models used for MPS deals, which the following two models are among the most popular. The first is commonly referred to as Utility billing model, something I briefly mentioned earlier. The second is Base + CPP (Cost per Page) billing model. The reason I want to discuss these two billing models is to give you an appreciation for the different revenue and cost implications each can have on the Deal P&L forecast. Furthermore, it's important to be aware each billing model presents varying levels of risk/opportunity for both the client and the MSP. Incidentally, MSPs use different names for these two common billing models. What they are called is not nearly as important as how they work, which I am about to explain.

Let's start with the Utility billing model, which clients simply pay for actual printed pages. As straightforward as that is from both a client billing and revenue recognition standpoint, the MSP gross margin can be extremely volatile because so much of the cost structure in Utility deals is fixed. Let's consider one of the MSPs' major fixed cost items, namely, embedded hardware lease payments. Keep in mind, the payment obligation the MSP (lessee) has to the financing company (lessor) is the same each month, regardless of whether the client prints 1,000 or 10,000 pages on a given device. In which case, the impact on MSP revenue can be significantly negative or positive, depending on which end of the volume spectrum actual printed pages fall. Stated differently, if the client prints quantities that are significantly below the solution assumption level, the MSP P&L will suffer the consequences. On the other hand, if actual printed quantities are significantly higher than the solution assumption, the MSP P&L will benefit. Incidentally, besides lease payments, the MSP will likely incur additional fixed service costs for such things as: dedicated client manager, delivery manager, operations and/or finance manager, and any other dedicated deal resources. In any case, the Deal Solution P&L (POR) is generally structured to recover all fixed costs, on the condition actual print volume is reasonably close to the solution volume assumption.

Now, let's talk briefly about Utility deals variable costs. Aside from supplies consumption cost, there are several variable service costs associated with Utility deals. Those costs include varying levels of: cross-charges for shared resources, on-site service incidents, vendor support cost, and more. Naturally, supplies and variable service costs are expected to be progressively higher as actual print volume increases. That's okay, since margin generated from incremental revenue should offset the higher variable costs. Therefore, the risk associated with Utility deals essentially comes down to whether or not fixed costs will be recovered. And, that risk rests totally with the MSP. Whereas, for the client, Utility deals are essentially risk-free.

In a Base + CPP billing model, there are two components that make up the monthly billing amount, which include a fixed per hardware unit component and a variable per printed page component. The fixed (or base) component contains two sub-components. One is the service sub-component, which billing is based on the number and type of hardware devices in the installed base. The other sub-component is the indirect payback for leased hardware. Although the end-client is technically not considered the lessee in an embedded lease arrangement, they are nevertheless indirectly responsible for the hardware lease payments. In other words, paying for the lease via the bundled MSP billing. In which case, neither of the above-mentioned fixed billing sub-components represent a risk for the MSP. The reason being, the client is obligated to pay those fixed amounts regardless of actual print volumes.

With regard to the variable billing component of Base + CPP deals, that too represents little risk for the MSP. The reason being, as print volume fluctuates, so too does the billing amount. In which case, as revenue goes up or down, the corresponding margin should fall in line with variable cost, essentially making the variable billing component margin neutral. Bottom line, between the two popular billing models we just discussed, Base + CPP is clearly the safer and lower risk model for the MSP. Conversely, they are more risky for the client, since the client is obligated to pay the fixed billing portion, regardless of actual print volumes.

Now that we've gotten the contracted billing models explanation out of the way, let's move on to actually forecasting supplies, starting with revenue. In both Utility and Base + CPP deals, one need only consider projected printed pages. Meaning, the more or less printed pages, the higher or lower the corresponding revenue forecast. To create the supplies revenue forecast, you would typically consider four variables, including: 1) normal run-rate billing; 2) seasonality in the client's business; 3) impact from projected print device ads and removals; and 4) billing anomalies. The first two variables are generally relatively easier to forecast; therefore, we will not discuss them further. Whereas, the last two categories are typically more difficult to forecast. Let's first consider projected device ads and removals to/from the installed base. As mentioned earlier in the hardware forecasting section, projecting the actual timing of device ads can be challenging. The basic reason, the client has greater control over the physical environment the devices are being placed than does the MSP. That means the latter is essentially at the mercy of the former, which is the reason respectful and diplomatic client/vendor relationships are so important.

From my personal experience, I'd have to say forecasting the impact of anomalies is the most challenging variable. Allow me to explain why that is. Anomalies represent unusual and oftentimes extraordinary spikes or drops in run-rate billing. That's true for anomalies that have already occurred, as well as those that are projected to occur in the future. In either case, in order for the P&L owner to create a reliable forecast, he needs to have a good grasp on what's going on in the client's environment. Let's first consider anomalies that have already occurred. Assume there was a $75,000 supplies billing spike in month 2 of the current fiscal year. The spike was due to 5 months retroactive billing for device ads that occurred toward the end of the prior fiscal year. Given the typical paperwork processing lag time that occurs in most businesses, this scenario is not at all uncommon. Let's assume further that month 3 just closed and you're in the process of creating a total year forecast. One of the most common mistakes that occur forecasting recurring revenue streams like supplies is simply doing run-rate forecasting without looking back at prior months details. Needless to say, this mindless approach will more often than not lead to inaccurate and unreliable forecasts.

I'm going to run through some numbers now, so please stay with me. Let's assume the normal supplies run-rate billing for this particular deal was $100,000/month prior to the one-time retroactive billing adjustment that occurred in month 2. If the forecasting was done properly, the total year revenue estimate would have been $1,410,000, which would have been calculated as follows: $100,000 for each month 1 and 2, plus $175,000 for month 3, plus $115,000 for each month 4 – 12. The reason for the $115,000 future monthly amount, the $75,000 five months back billing would have added $15,000/month to the base revenue.

On the other hand, if the forecast was done improperly (based on year-to-date run-rate), the total year forecast would have been $1,500,000, which would have been calculated as follows: $375,000 for months 1 – 3 combined, plus $125,000 for each month 4 – 12. The $125,000/month was derived from dividing actual year-to-date revenue of $375,000 by 3. This erroneous approach would have resulted in $90,000 total year forecasting error. Although that may not sound like much, if the numbers were actually higher than the given example, or there were several other accounts in the portfolio that experienced similar back-billing situations, it's easy to see how the cumulative effect could result in a significant forecasting error.

Now let's look at the impact a *projected* billing anomaly would have on supplies revenue forecast. In this case, the most common mistake that occurs is not taking into account the impact the one-time projected billing adjustment will have on future months. In this example, let's assume once again the run-rate billing before adjustment is $100,000/month, and there is a one-time $75,000 billing adjustment projected to occur in month 6. Here again, let's assume we just closed month 3, and we are in the process of creating a total year forecast. If you do not think carefully about the impact to future months, you might mistakenly forecast $1,275,000 for the total year, which is calculated as follows: $100,000 for each month 1 – 5 and month 7 – 12, plus $175,000 for month 6.

Obviously, the one-time $75,000 billing adjustment will also impact future recurring revenue. Assuming the billing adjustment impacts 5 backdated months means future billing (beyond month 6) will increase by $15,000/month. In which case, the correct total year revenue forecast would be $1,365,000, which is calculated as follows: $100,000 for each month 1 – 5, plus $175,000 for month 6, plus $115,000 for each month 7 – 12. Here again, the wrong approach would have resulted in a total year forecasting error of $90,000. The take away from the two given examples, impact from both past and projected anomalies must be normalized in order to create a reliable forecast.

Supplies cost forecasting for both Utility and Base + CPP billing models can be extremely difficult if you're attempting to achieve an absolute match between revenue and cost. Since billing is based on actual number of printed pages, estimating the corresponding amount of toner consumed in each cartridge in hundreds or maybe thousands of printers in the client's environment is impractical and virtually impossible. Therefore, the next best thing is to base the supplies cost forecast on the relationship between historical toner shipped to actual number of printed pages. Once you have a good handle on the shipments to pages relationship, you should be able to develop a reasonably accurate supplies cost forecast that is based on projected number of printed pages.

Depending on the deal specific circumstances, you may be required to make some adjustments to the forecast calculation for some other known conditions. For example, customers who are allowed to draw from locally stocked client specific inventory. In those cases, changes in local stocking levels must also be considered in the supplies cost forecast, which of course makes the process a bit more challenging. Bottom line, don't drive yourself crazy trying to achieve absolute accuracy. Given the fact that achieving an absolute match between revenue and cost is practically impossible, close enough is good enough for supplies cost forecasting.

Last but certainly not least, let's talk about forecasting the services portion of a Deal P&L, once again starting with revenue. As with supplies, the service revenue forecast is heavily influenced by the contracted billing model. As stated earlier, for Utility deals everything that is billed to the client is based on printed pages. Therefore, forecasted service revenue is strictly based on projected printed pages. Meaning, the higher/lower the projected printed pages, the higher/lower will be the service revenue forecast. Beyond that basic cause and effect relationship, the same four variables mentioned in the supplies revenue forecasting section must also be considered in the services revenue forecast. To reiterate, those variables include: 1) normal run-rate billing; 2) seasonality in the client's business; 3) impact from projected print device ads and removals; and 4) billing anomalies.

For Base + CPP billing model, service is part of the base billing. Therefore, the single most important factor that influences the service revenue forecast is the number and type of hardware units in the client's environment. If changes are anticipated in the client's physical environment, so too must the impact of those charges be reflected in the service revenue forecast. Beyond that, you have to normalize run-rate billing by considering the impact from any past and/or anticipated future anomalies, as described in the supplies revenue forecasting section.

Without question, projecting the service cost is the most challenging aspect of MPS deal forecasting. As with many cost categories, service cost involves both a fixed and a variable component. The fixed component, which is relatively easier to forecast, includes such things as salary for the following dedicated deal resources: client manager, delivery manager, operations manager, finance manager, and any number of other dedicated specialty resources that are required to support the deal. Beyond that, other fixed costs might include amortization of capitalized initial start-up cost, which is quite common, particularly in bigger deals. Specifically, I am referring to capitalized up-front discovery, design, and deployment costs. Fixed costs could also include recurring software license and maintenance fees for third party software required in the deal. Depending on the specific deal and circumstances, there may be some additional fixed service cost items that must be considered in the forecast. Nevertheless, the items mentioned are among the most common big ticket items.

Forecasting variable service cost is unquestionably more challenging than forecasting fixed cost. There are three principal reasons. First, most MPS deals utilize shared resources, some more than others. Furthermore, for any number of reasons, shared resource charges for a given deal can vary significantly from month to month. As mentioned earlier, most deals experience the highest level of shared resource charges in the early stage of contract life, when design and hardware deployment occur. Second, the number of on-site service incidents and related parts consumption for a given deal can likewise vary significantly from month to month. And third, applicable vendor support cost can also fluctuate from month to month. Noteworthy, accounting for vendor support cost often involves booking accruals and accrual reversals, which are required due to timing differences between when services are rendered versus paid. That too must be considered in the service cost forecast. As you can see from the few given examples, forecasting variable service cost can be quite involved. Therefore, the more you know about the intricacies of the deal and the client's environment, the higher the probability of producing a reliable forecast.

Forecasting Tools

The distinction between forecasting processes and tools, the former defines the *how to*, whereas, the latter is the enabler that makes creating a forecast possible. Without an accompanying tool, forecasting is likely to be tediously manual and extraordinarily time consuming. On the other hand, the best tools alone will not guarantee the creation of high-quality forecasts. Creating reliable forecasts requires a combination of well-defined processes, tools, and most importantly knowledgeable and business-savvy people. You cannot simply hand over to a P&L owner a forecasting process document and a slick tool, and expect them to generate reliable forecasts. I've seen this approach tried and fail time and again. The fact of the matter, everyone comes into a new P&L owner position with different experiences and skill sets. Some may have prior P&L management and forecasting experience, while others have little or none of either.

So, if you want to make sure all P&L owners do a respectable job managing their respective Deal P&L and produce reliable forecasts, you have to invest in training those people, particularly the less experienced individuals. For some individuals, that may mean providing some basic pre-requisite financial management training. For others, it may mean providing a deeper understanding of how business transactions drive the business financials, etc. Once everyone has achieved at least a baseline understanding of Finance fundamentals, you can then proceed with introducing forecasting process and tools training. It takes time and requires management patience to do it right.

P&L forecasting tools vary anywhere from basic spreadsheets to robust and integrated application systems. In either case, understanding the tool mechanics, as well as the intricacies of the business, are essential pre-requisites to producing sound business forecasts. Generally speaking, the more sophisticated and integrated the forecasting tool, the fewer user inputs required. The reason being, algorithms built into automated tools will automatically handle multiple layers of calculations derived from minimal user inputs, while also essentially eliminating calculation errors. Conversely, calculation errors are precisely what you need to be most concerned when creating forecasts on non-automated tools. Automated tools are also typically programmed to systematically handle the impact on downstream P&L components. For example, with proper built-in algorithm, all you need to do is input hardware adds/removals/changes, and the tool will automatically calculate the impact on related consumables and services revenue and cost forecast.

Let me give you a vivid example of what I am referring. Assume you are forecasting an MPS deal. Regardless of whether you are using a manual spreadsheet or an automated tool, there would typically be four sheets included in the manual workbook or automated tool. One sheet for the total P&L forecast, and one sheet each for hardware, supplies, and service component forecast. As previously mentioned, hardware drives the other two downstream components, namely, supplies and services. Therefore, by simply imputing hardware adds/removals/changes into the automated tool will automatically calculate and populate the applicable supplies and service cells, based on pre-defined user parameters. In other words, the user can choose to base the annuity component forecast on, let's say, the average revenue and cost values for the past 3, 6, or 12 months.

Furthermore, the user can define the average amount of time after hardware shipment the annuity revenue and cost will commence. Ultimately, the automated calculations generate a so called *placeholder forecast*. In other words, a system generated preliminary forecast. Afterward, the P&L owner can manually override any of those pre-populated cells to reflect known deal specifics such as impact from seasonality, anomalies, etc. Once the tweaking is completed, the forecast is considered final. At which point, the P&L owner will formally submit the forecast to management, and will subsequently be held accountable for achieving corresponding actual results.

Summary

Recap of Key Points and Takeaways

At this point, I'd like to do a recap of the key points we discussed, along with recommended takeaways. Before we start, I'd like to share some thoughts about the different approaches used to tackle profit improvement opportunities. Some people believe it is best to tackle the more challenging items first. Based on the assumption, less challenging items are either not worth pursuing, or they will go away when the big items have been successfully addressed. Other people treat essentially all challenges as priority #1. Considering the fact most companies are dealing with limited resources that have limited available cycles, addressing several items simultaneously is simply not practical in most cases. Other people prefer tackling low-hanging fruit first. Still others may prefer using some other more scientific or mathematical approach used to select high priority items. The fact of the matter, there is no one right approach. It basically comes down to what management believes works best for their company and provides optimal results.

From my experience, I have found that tackling low-hanging fruit first usually works best, regardless of whether those items are considered big or small. When I say small, I am not referring to minutia level small. Obviously, there is no point tackling insignificant value items, assuming of course the underlining objective is improving profitability. In any case, there are a couple of reasons why this approach has proven widely successful. One, the impact to bottom line financials is immediate. And two, there is nothing better to help get the juices flowing (so to speak) than immediately establishing winning momentum.

Now let's start our recap. Unlike most businesses, MPS Deal Pursuit (or Sales) cycles are generally lengthy and costly, and involve intense competition. Therefore, the Deal Solution team will do everything reasonably possible to remain in a competitive pursuit. Unfortunately, that often means agreeing to deliverables the delivery organization is not equipped to handle without introducing one-off processes, which can be costly and cumbersome. An alternative that sometimes works with motivated clients, is offering them a lower price for accepting standard deliverables, which can potentially benefit both the client and the MSP.

Discovery represents the first physical action the MSP undertakes when pursuing an MPS deal. Generally speaking, there are two discovery phases involved in most MPS deals. The first is a pre-contract discovery, which is typically limited to 10 - 25% of the client's total environment. The locations that initial discovery is done can have a significant impact on the final agreement. The reason being, a misrepresentative sample of the client's current environment can result in misguided solution assumptions, which will ultimately result in a faulty Solution P&L. Generally speaking, the larger and more representative the pre-contract discovery sample, the more reliable will likely be the Solution P&L. Post-signing discovery, which involves inspecting the client's remaining existing environment, is essentially unimportant from a Solution P&L standpoint. The reason being, any potential damage that may have been done would likely be the result of a non-representative pre-contract discovery sample.

Like discovery, design is also critically important. The two most important aspects of design are hardware placement, which takes into account optimal device type, size, and location, and limiting the client's direct involvement in the design process. The fact of the matter, the more involved the client is with design, the longer and more costly you can expect the process to be. The reason being, when clients are involved, there are usually more design revisions, and the decision-making process is considerably slower than it would be otherwise. It may be challenging to convince your client to agree to a *hands-off* approach. Nevertheless, if you can get your client to agree to hands-off, it's definitely the best and most efficient way to go.

With regard to deployment, sometimes it goes flawlessly and other times it's mired with challenges. Two of the biggest challenges related to deployment are product availability and site readiness. Although it's difficult to avoid inherent product availability issues, there are ways the transition manager can work around those problems. One way is to willingly accept partial instead of complete shipments when products are on allocation. That way, everyone seeking those limited products feels a little pain, instead of some being completely satisfied at the cost of others who receive no product at all. Reasonableness and diplomacy are key in these situations. Butting heads with hardware sourcing personnel will almost never pay off. With regard to site readiness, the transition manager is essentially at the client's mercy. Here again, being reasonable and diplomatic with the client will always produce better results than butting heads. Nevertheless, if you have determined the matter needs to be escalated to keep deployment on schedule, do so with care and respect.

Steady state is by far the longest segment of an MPS deal. Therefore, how efficient and effective this segment is handled is hugely important to the overall success and profitability of the deal. One of the most critical aspects of steady state is client relationship management. Incidentally, that does not mean you have to unconditionally agree to all of the client's wishes. Some customers will test you by continuing to push until you say "stop." The best relationship you can have with a client is one of mutual respect and a balance of give and take. Lopsided relationships, one way or the other, will almost never work. There is one additional major item that needs to be addressed concerning steady state, which is related to on-site hardware service and support. Regardless of whether on-site service is being provided by an internal or external service provider, a formal agreement between the two parties is highly recommended. Without such an agreement, the MSP is potentially exposed to a significant amount of unnecessary risk.

With regard to the overhead functions we discussed in the detailed writing, including Business Ops, Business Analysis, and Global Functions, there is only one critical thing I'd like to reiterate. The cost versus value of overhead resources needs to constantly be reevaluated. Otherwise, instead of helping the business generate profit, those resources will consume profit.

In essentially every business, managing clients, vendors, and assets is equally important to managing the internal organization. Managing some MPS clients is a delight, while managing some other clients is challenging to say the least. Even though an MPS portfolio may have a few small/medium challenging deals, it's the large multinational deals that are typically the most challenging. The primary reason, those clients are experts in vendor management. Even during the deal bidding process, they know how to effectively play vendors against one another to obtain the best possible solution and price. It's not unusual for those very same clients to continually challenge the MSP throughout the life of the deal seeking price reductions and/or concessions. Therefore, it's important for the MSP to respectfully stand their ground with those clients. Otherwise, they will take advantage of the MSP, and the Deal P&L will suffer the consequences. On the other hand, it's the small\medium deals with standard deliverables that are easier to manage and more profitable than large complex deals, which competing vendors fight tooth and nail to win. Ironic, isn't it!

That's the price MSPs oftentimes pay for the privilege of having those big company logos included in their client list.

MSPs typically engage with resource vendors for one or more of the following reasons: gain access to specialty resources, obtain temporary resources needed to augment internal capabilities, and engage with low-cost service providers. Additionally, MSPs often utilize other vendor software/solutions that are bundled into end-client deliverables. All things considered, for MSPs that cannot leverage an internal service organization, their most significant vendor cost will likely be for on-site service. Regardless of whether the MSP utilizes an internal and/or external on-site service provider, there should always be incentives to minimize the number of on-site dispatches. The obvious reason, fewer dispatches equate to lower on-site service cost.

In MPS businesses, managing contracted deal related assets is particularly important. In this case, I am referring to hardware devices that are funded via embedded leases, which is quite common in MPS deals. Although ownership of those assets technically remains with the leasing entity, the MSP has financial responsibility for managing the assets. Therefore, it's important for the MSP to ensure all leased assets are accounted for and in use. Otherwise, they will be obligated to continue paying for unused assets, even though they are not receiving any revenue benefit from the end-client.

For the most part, service is a people intensive business, which means the most significant investment made by service organizations is typically on human resources. Regardless of whether you are dealing with existing, replacement, or additional resources, oftentimes there are shortcomings associated with human resource justification. The biggest shortcoming usually being lack of consistent process rigor.

With regard to existing resources, most companies do not bother to re-justify them each year. Instead, those resources are automatically baked into the baseline budget, which could very well represent a missed cost reduction opportunity. With regard to replacement resource justification, a different kind of problem often comes into play. Specifically, the flawed notion, if there was good reason for having the position filled before it was vacated, there is good reason to backfill the position. Instead, managers should view every vacated position as an opportunity to potentially reduce operating cost. In many cases, that can be done by eliminating non-essential activities the departed resource handled, and distributing the remaining activities to other existing resources. In other cases, there may be an opportunity to lower the vacated job level, which may have been unduly influenced by the seniority of the incumbent. Instead of automatically filling the vacated position with the same job level, managers should consider paying for the actual knowledge and skills required to do the job. With regard to additional resource justification, the biggest issue I have seen is justification that is need (or faith) based, instead of based on quantified value. Although I am a proponent of quantified value justification, there are situations that approach is simply not practical or possible. In those cases, the least that should be done is after the fact evaluation to assess whether or not a financially prudent decision was actually made hiring the additional resource.

In Managed Services businesses, direct labor resources are typically categorized as either being dedicated or shared, meaning they are either dedicated to a single deal or support multiple deals. The cost capture and accounting for dedicated versus shared resources is very different. Cost for a dedicated resource is simply assigned to the dedicated deal cost center, and subsequently reflected on the corresponding Deal P&L. Whereas, cost capture and accounting for a shared resource is more involved. Initially, the shared resource cost is posted to the cost center the individual is assigned. For example, a shared deployment resource would be assigned to a Deployment

Management cost center. With the use of a Labor Tracking & Costing system, which records hours worked by each shared resource on each deal, labor cost is transferred from shared cost centers to the appropriate deal cost centers, and subsequently reflected on the corresponding Deal P&Ls.

Labor Tracking & Costing tools are invaluable from the standpoint of handling labor cost capture and allocation, as well as measuring and managing individual utilization. However, if you are attempting to improve direct labor resource utilization, there are additional factors that come into play. One very important factor is standardization, which most Managed Services businesses attempt to maximize wherever reasonably possible in order to maximize profitability. On the other hand, one of the struggles Managed Services delivery organizations typically face is dealing with ever-increasing non-standard deliverables resulting from competitive deal solutions. Needless to say, Sales and Solution teams should do everything reasonably possible to contain non-standard deliverables. One very effective way of doing so is offering clients incentives (financial or otherwise) to discourage them from insisting on non-standard deliverables. Other important factors that can and should be leveraged to maximize resource utilization include training and development, as well as streamlining business processes. Leveraging some or all of the above-mentioned factors can go a long way to improve resource utilization and contribute to profit maximization.

With the exception of small mom and pop operations, indirect labor (or overhead) resources are essential in most businesses. It's hard to imagine running a viable business without Management, Finance, Human Resources, Legal, etc. Therefore, the question regarding overhead resources is not whether to have them or not. It's really a question about how many are required and justifiable on the basis of cost versus return value. Unfortunately, most companies do not approach indirect resource hiring decisions with payback value in mind, which is the principal reason so many companies end up having more indirect resources than can be economically justified. Furthermore, growth in indirect resources is oftentimes linear with growth in business, which is not prudent for efficiently run businesses. With growth, businesses will almost certainly have to add indirect resources. However, along with growth should come more efficiency, not more waste.

A fundamental question that should always be asked when making resource decisions: is it better to use external or internal resources? For the most part, a decision whether or not to go with external resources comes down to two primary considerations, namely economics and risk. With regard to the economic aspect, you must be careful to consider all of the related internal and external cost factors in order to produce a true *apples-to-apples* comparison. With regard to risk, it comes down to the company's risk tolerance and their ability to remain cost/price competitive. Risk generally represents a balancing act between rewards and consequences, measured in terms of dollars and impact on customer satisfaction. Shrinking global markets and ever-increasing competitive pressures are forcing business managers to constantly reevaluate their resource strategy, and oftentimes make unpopular decisions regarding the use of external resources.

Taking advantage of low-cost offshore resources is enticing, especially for companies that are attempting to either preserve or improve profitability. However, it's also important to acknowledge there are inherent risks associated with offshoring. Meaning it will not always prove to be the best or most cost-effective choice. At first glance, offshoring will almost always be appealing because it provides access to low-cost resources. However, unless there is considerable effort and care applied to the planning, design, and rollout of the offshore solution, the cost advantage can quickly disappear. Invariably, the single biggest challenge associated with successful offshoring is quality control, and the second biggest challenge is dealing with high attrition rates. In developing countries where wages are low and competition for low-cost resources is high, people often move from company to company for marginally better wages.

From a best practices standpoint, external resource agreements should always include clearly defined deliverables and performance goals. When external resources are hired by a middleman such as an MSP, the deliverables and performance goals the MSP is accountable to the end-client must also be reflected in the contractual agreement between the external resource vendor and the MSP. That way, both parties share responsibility for achieving end-client deliverables, as well as any potentially applicable non-performance penalties.

In business, profitability is measured and managed from multiple aspects. Depending on the size and scope of the business, in addition to a total company P&L, there are P&Ls created for each of the countries and regions the business operates. In contracted service businesses, it's equally important to create individual Deal P&Ls. Typically, there are three different Deal P&L views, including Plan of Record, Actuals, and Forecast.

The Plan of Record or POR P&L reflects the final approved contracted deal. That P&L is considered to be the all-important point of reference that Actual and Forecast Deal P&Ls are measured against throughout the entire life of the deal. There are several factors considered in a deal approval process, including deal size and scope, client strategic importance, and more. However, how good or bad the Deal POR P&L looks is typically the single most important factor that determines whether or not a deal will be approved.

In highly competitive MPS deals, the biggest deals usually have the lowest gross margin. The reason being, MSPs typically fight tooth and nail to win big deals. Why, you might ask? Sometimes it's because they are trying to rapidly grow the top line. Other times they may be trying to penetrate a particular business sector, etc. Admittedly, there may be some differentiating qualities and/or capabilities amongst competitors. However, for the most part, MPS has become a commodity business with more or less standard products and solutions. Therefore, winning essentially comes down to price. But here's the thing. When an MSP wins one of these big deals, who really is the winner, the MSP or the client? I contend it's usually the savvy client who knows how to effectively play competitors against one another to get the best deal for the lowest possible price. And, most times the loser is the MSP who won the deal. The reason being, the MSP typically ends up owning a complicated, low margin deal, which they have to attentively manage throughout the entire life of the deal to potentially squeeze some profit out of the deal.

The fact of the matter, low margin revenue has never and will never help a company achieve long-term financial success. Sure, some of those deals can be turned around, but not without a tremendous amount of effort and oversight. Therefore, the question becomes, was it really worth it? The take away here, be careful not to load up your deal portfolio with too many of these big low margin deals. The reason being, your deal portfolio will unlikely be able to withstand the resulting margin pressure, which incidentally is typically offset by respectable margins generated from standard small/medium deals.

One of the major challenges associated with Deal POR P&Ls, they often reflect unrealistic and unattainable gross margins. In which case, Deal P&L owners usually end up being victim to highly competitive and poorly conceived deal solutions. The bigger the deal, the more intense the competition, and more pressure there is on gross margin. In order to win these large competitive deals, the Solution team has to be very aggressive. Translated, that usually means the numbers reflected in the POR P&L represents best case scenario, which rarely turns out to be reality. Furthermore, as competition intensifies, the Solution team will typically make progressively more unrealistic assumptions.

Once the deal is rolled out, all the assumptions that were made by the Solution team (good or bad) rest squarely on the shoulders of the Deal P&L owner, which is typically the delivery or client manager. Meanwhile, the Solution team gets to walk away with kudos for winning the deal, along with corresponding incentive compensation. There is only one way to effectively address this problem. Delay a significant portion of the Solution team incentive compensation until actual versus plan financial performance has been assessed for a reasonable period of time after the deal rollout. In the detailed writing, I suggested a couple of different ways to do that. Bottom line, the best way to affect the Solution team behavior is by affecting their personal wallets.

Actual Deal P&Ls provide both a historical view regarding deal profitability, as well as a means for measuring actual performance against POR. In MPS businesses, managing individual deal financial performance is every bit as important as managing the deal portfolio performance for two reasons. First, just because your total portfolio may be performing well, does not necessarily mean each individual deal in the portfolio is doing likewise. Second, without individual Deal P&Ls, there is no way of knowing what's working in accordance with the original plan and what's not working. When we think about Actual Deal P&Ls, it's crucial to be mindful of three important points. First, reliable Deal P&Ls start and end with financial integrity. Second, you can't fix something you don't have a good understanding of transaction source data. Third, it is imperative that you have a good handle on business drivers. Beyond that, there is essentially only one other thing the account manager should be concerned, increasing deal size and scope while maintaining or improving customer satisfaction.

P&Ls that lack integrity can be misleading and potentially dangerous, since many business decisions are influenced by P&L results. Data integrity is not something that accidentally happens. It only exists when businesses are supported by sound processes and procedures, complemented with clear and concise employee communications and training. From a deal revenue standpoint, one of the most important factors that influences integrity is the accuracy of customer master data. From a deal cost standpoint, getting account coding and cost center structure right are two of the most important factors that affect integrity.

There are two fundamental ways of getting cost reflected in a Deal P&L, either on an actual transaction basis or allocation basis. The more cost is allocated, the less accurate you should expect the Deal P&Ls to be. Furthermore, one sure way of avoiding deal cost complications, is setting up a dedicated cost center in the General Ledger for each contracted deal. That way, you're essentially guaranteed to capture all deal related costs in the intended cost bucket. In addition, wherever possible, you will want to automate sub-system feeds. For example, automate the feed from the service application system to the General Ledger. The more automation that exists, the quicker your Deal P&Ls will be available and more accurate they will be.

As the saying goes, you can't fix something you don't understand. That is precisely why having a good understanding of transaction source data is critically important to effectively manage and control deal profitability. For the most part, source business and financial data is derived from one or more of the following: integrated reporting databases, individual application system databases, and manual transactions such as journal entries and spreadsheets.

The more automated and integrated the database solution, the more efficient and better quality will be the reported data. Furthermore, you have to have a reasonably good understanding of business drivers that affect deal profitability. The reason being, data alone is essentially meaningless. Source data must be routinely reviewed for accuracy, anomalies, and potential errors, followed by taking timely and appropriate action to address any questionable data. Ignoring transaction source data because it's too tedious for you or someone else in your organization to review allows unnoticed problems to fester, which are almost guaranteed to adversely affect your Deal P&L.

In the detailed writing, I filled quite a number of pages talking about business drivers and improving profitability by leveraging available levers and knobs. I believe the subject matter is important, and therefore warranted that much discussion. Business drivers mean different things to different people, and can include any number of both internal and external factors that impact deal revenue and cost. As a Deal P&L owner, if you do nothing to influence those business drivers, like it or not, you will have to live with the resulting P&L.

On the other hand, if you take control and manage available levers and knobs, your deal financial performance is almost guaranteed to improve. You should think about these levers and knobs much like tools in your home toolbox. In which case, if a screw comes loose in one of your wooden kitchen chairs, you pull out the appropriate type and size screwdriver to tighten the screw to make the chair stable and safe again. Business levers and knobs work essentially the same way. There are a number of them available, just like the different tools in your toolbox. It's just a matter of selecting the right tool for the task at hand. The only difference, instead of fixing a broken chair, you're fixing a broken deal.

And now, let's do a quick recap of growing existing deal scope and size, which is typically handled by the delivery or client manager via the Charge Order process. Basically, that means those individuals have to keep their eyes and ears opened for any and all relatively significant business expansion opportunities. That said, nitpicking with your client is not smart. Meaning, it's not a good idea to stick a Change Order under your client's nose every time they ask for the slightest thing not covered under the contract. On the other hand, neither is giving away what could otherwise generate incremental revenue. My point being, don't be apprehensive or overly aggressive presenting your client with Change Orders. Also, it's always wise for the MSP to establish guidelines for deal managers to follow regarding the appropriate use of Change Orders. Incidentally, Change Orders are typically more profitable than contracted in-scope work, which makes them especially important from a margin contribution perspective. Bottom line, don't leave high margin incremental revenue on the table that is rightfully yours to claim.

P&L forecasting is as much an art form as it is a science, which accuracy and reliability improves with training and experience. The science is leveraging currently available data to predict what is likely to happen in the future. The art form is applying learned skills to produce a reasonably accurate and clear view of future business outcome. It's not just the person's forecasting abilities and learned skills that matter. Equally important is the level of business acumen one possesses. There are a number of factors that typically influence the quality of a forecast, such as the external environment, seasonality, etc. For MPS Deal P&L forecasting, there are more factors that must be considered, such as hardware conversion, stage in the contract life cycle, etc. Taking all these factors and more into account will ultimately influence the quality and reliability of your forecast.

At its core, forecasting is a business management responsibility that encompasses two major components, processes and tools. Furthermore, business forecasting is distinct from financial forecasting. In which case, the latter essentially represents aggregated views of the former. Ultimately, the one thing that matters most is forecasting accuracy, which represents a measurement of how close historical forecasts have been to actual results. The process aspect of forecasting is not something you can simply diagram a flowchart, and hand it over to someone to create a forecast. For the most part, forecasting is a learned skill that usually improves with training and experience. Aside from learning how to effectively use the company's forecasting tool, there are some foundational knowledge requirements one must possess before they can be expected to produce a sound and reliable forecast. First and foremost, he must have a good understanding of financial implications resulting from business transactions. Equally important, he must have a good grasp of business drivers, meaning, when a specific business event occurs, what can reasonably be expected to follow, and when is that follow-on action likely to occur.

Some businesses are easier to forecast than others. For example, forecasting a distribution business is relatively straightforward, especially when customers provide demand forecasts. On the other hand, forecasting an MPS business is much more complicated, due to the number of variables that can affect the P&L forecast, particularly items the service provider has little or no control, such as readiness of the client's environment.

While forecasting processes define the *how to*, forecasting tools are the enabler. Those tools vary from rudimentary spreadsheets to sophisticated integrated application systems. The latter normally contain built-in formulas and algorithms that minimize user input requirements to create a so-called *placeholder* forecast, which can subsequently be manually tweaked by the P&L owner. Once the desired adjustments have been made, the P&L owner will submit the final forecast to management and Finance, and subsequently be held accountable for achieving the forecasted results. I'd like to make one final comment regarding forecasting processes and tools. It's important to be mindful that the best processes and tools alone will not guarantee accurate and reliable forecasts. You will also have to invest in foundational training to ensure all your P&L owners possess at least baseline forecasting knowledge and skills.

At this point, I'd like to make a few closing comments. Regardless of the reason you picked up and decided to read this book, I hope you found it beneficial in some way or another. For those of you who are involved in a service business (whether it's MPS or otherwise), your own experiences can now be coupled with the experiences I have shared. Without question, learning from one's own experience is always best. Second best is learning from someone else's shared experience, which was precisely my intent writing this book. For those of you who are not involved in a service business, but maybe aspire to do so in the future, this book may serve as a good *jump start*. And finally, for those of you who were simply drawn to the book because the title caught your eye, welcome to the world of services. For me, it's personally gratifying to know that I've shared information that may somehow be useful and beneficial to others.

Before signing off, I'd like to offer one final piece of advice. Taking advantage of the many profit improvement ideas I shared is a good thing. On the other hand, taking advantage of your clients is not. Just as I preached about the importance of return value throughout the book, customers expect the same for money they spend on products and services. Once they sense their vendor has taken advantage of them, you can say goodbye to those customers. Getting them back or finding replacement customers is almost guaranteed to be more costly than the incremental profit you may have generated from unscrupulous business practices. Be fair and respectful to all of your customers, and they will be loyal in return. In service businesses, customer loyalty is one of the most important keys to success.

www.ingramcontent.com/pod-product-compliance
Lightning Source LLC
Chambersburg PA
CBHW051458170526
45166CB00001B/292